ADLAI STEVENSON'S PUBLIC YEARS

ADLAI STEVENSON'S PUBLIC YEARS

with text from his speeches and
writings, edited by Jill Kneerim

PHOTOGRAPHS *by*
CORNELL CAPA,
John Fell Stevenson & Inge Morath

Preface by Walter Lippmann

GROSSMAN PUBLISHERS   NEW YORK   1966

Copyright © 1966 by Grossman Publishers, Inc.
All photographs copyright 1952, © 1956, 1958,
1960, 1961 by Magnum Photos, Inc.
All rights reserved.
Excerpts from the introduction to Major Campaign Speeches 1952 *(copyright 1953 by Random House, Inc.) are condensed and reprinted with the permission of Random House; and the conversation with Khrushchev, taken from pages 3–12 of* Friends and Enemies *(copyright © 1958, 1959 by Adlai E. Stevenson), is reproduced with the permission of Harper and Row, Publishers.*

Published by Grossman Publishers, Inc.
125A East 19th Street, New York, New York
Manufactured in the United States of America
Library of Congress Catalog Card No: 66-19525
First Printing

This book could not have been produced without the cooperation of Life *magazine, of Magnum Photos, and of Adlai E. Stevenson III and John Fell Stevenson. A portion of the royalties from the sale of the book goes to the Adlai E. Stevenson Memorial Fund.*

Contents

In place of the usual ellipsis, this device ☐ serves to indicate deletions of a paragraph or more from the original text.

Preface

We must wonder whether we have buried with Adlai Stevenson some element of the promise of American life. For in this generation he has stood apart, not only for his deeds and his words and his wit and his lovableness, but as somehow a living specimen of the kind of American that Americans themselves, and the great mass of mankind, would like to think that Americans are.

He was not a common man or a typical American of our times or, indeed, of any other time. But he evoked for us the mystic chords of memory because he touched again "the better angels of our nature." From Lincoln to Adlai Stevenson the heritage is direct and unbroken, a family tradition which began with his great-grandfather. Like Lincoln, he made men feel what this nation had to be if the American experiment was to succeed. Like Lincoln, he was what the prairies and the New World had made of the educated Englishmen who led this country in the eighteenth century.

This Lincolnian American is, as compared with Washington or Jefferson, the first authentic American, the new man of the New World. Before Lincoln, the distinguished Americans were transplanted Englishmen. Since Lincoln, there has existed the idea of a special American type which is excellent and admirable and holds the promise of a better human future. Adlai Stevenson was a rare, perhaps a late-blooming, example of such an American. He was admired by the discerning all over the world and greatly loved. An essential ingredient of the admiration and the love was the knowledge that only America could have produced him, and that this revealed what America really was.

The question is now whether this country is still devoted to the American idea which he embodied. No one supposes, of course, that the country can be filled with Stevensons any more than a hundred years ago it was filled with Lincolns, any more than Britain is filled with Churchills. It is only occasionally and for a while that nations are represented by their greatest men. The question is whether, in our critical moments, the better angels of our nature respond to our authentic ideals.

For there is abroad in this land today a very different spirit contending for the soul of our people. The original American has had for a central idea, as Lincoln said at Gettysburg, that America was an experiment of consequence to all mankind and that, primarily, the influence of America was its example. The new spirit among us is imperious and assumes that our influence is measured by our money and our power.

The struggle between the two spirits has appeared and reappeared throughout our history. But, with the enormous and sudden increase of our power and wealth, the stress and strain of the struggle for the American soul has become fierce. It is the uncertainty as to which spirit will prevail that divides, more than tactics or manners or policy, the American people among themselves and from the world around us.

Adlai Stevenson's enemies were not men whom he had injured. He injured no men. His enemies were men who recognized that he did not share and was a living reproach to the new imperiousness of our power and wealth, that he was a deeply established American who had no part in the arrogance of the newly rich and the newly powerful and the newly arrived. His very presence made them uncomfortable, even abashed, all the more because he was so witty when they were so hot, so elegant when they were making a spectacle of themselves.

Shall we see his like again? Or was he the last of his noble breed? On this question hangs the American future. On one course we shall plunge ourselves into the making of a ramshackle empire in an era when no empire can long survive, and we shall wave the flag to cover our spiritual nakedness.

Or we shall, as Adlai Stevenson would have done, remain true to our original loyalty, and transcending assertiveness, vulgar ambition and the seductions of power, we shall make this country not only great and free but at peace with its own conscience.

—WALTER LIPPMANN

I

BEGINNINGS

On February 5, 1900, Adlai Ewing Stevenson II was born in Los Angeles. Six years later his family moved from California to Bloomington, Illinois, where Stevenson grew up. He was educated at the public schools there, except for one year with his family in Switzerland, and in 1916 he went east to Choate, thence to Princeton, and finally to Harvard Law School at the insistence of his father. After two years Stevenson left Harvard to help settle a family inheritance question involving the Bloomington Pantagraph, the town's newspaper. For the next two years he served as an editor and reporter on its staff, and for the rest of his life his part ownership of the paper brought him a reliable annual income.

Stevenson finished law school at Northwestern University in 1926 and was admitted to the bar in Illinois, but before beginning a law practice he took a last fling in the form of a trip to Russia, acting as a correspondent for the Pantagraph. When it became obvious that his audacious hope of becoming the first Western journalist to interview Soviet Foreign Minister Chicherin was unrealistic, he returned to Chicago and joined one of the city's old, established law firms. In 1928 he married Ellen Borden of Chicago, and in 1933 he was offered his first job in Washington, D.C.

AN EDUCATION IN POLITICS *From Stevenson's introduction to his first book,* Major Campaign Speeches, 1952, *published by Random House in 1953.*

My father's family moved to Kentucky from Virginia and North Carolina, and a generation or so later, they moved on to Bloomington, Illinois, before the Civil War. They were Scotch-Irish Presbyterians and Democrats, and strong in the faith, both political and religious. Miraculously, Grandfather Stevenson flourished politically in Republican Illinois and was elected Vice-President with Grover Cleveland in 1892. He was nominated again with Bryan in 1900, and, as a feeble old man, was a reluctant but very strong candidate for Governor in 1908. My father's Democratic allegiance and activity ended only with his death in 1929.

But my mother's family were Pennsylvania Quakers who came early to Illinois. Her grandfather, Jesse Fell, was a "liberal" of those days, I suppose, an abolitionist, educator and a founder of the Unitarian church in Bloomington. Discontented with the Whigs, he took the leading part in organizing a Republican party in central Illinois and worked tirelessly for the advancement of his long-time friend, Abraham Lincoln. His son-in-law, my grandfather, William Osborn Davis, was also a Pennsylvania Quaker who found the Unitarian church in Bloomington much to his liking. For forty years he was a leading Republican editor and publisher of Illinois.

So it is hardly surprising that, when the son of the Democratic Vice-President married the daughter of the Republican editor of the same town, the newspapers of the country headlined the event as a "triumph of love over politics."

Small wonder, then, that as I grew up in Bloomington, I found myself in Mother's beloved Unitarian church and Father's beloved Democratic party. I guess I was a compromise to begin with, which may have predestined a political career for which I had no conscious stomach, and, I might add, no positive encouragement from my father at any time.

There was little of black and white in our home as I look back on it. Visiting the two grandfathers on Sundays and vacations, I was often in Presbyterian churches and saw and listened to as many articulate Republicans as Democrats, perhaps more, because the local Democrats were few—but hardy!—in Bloomington in those days.

Thinking of political influences brings back one unhappy incident of those days. It was a Sunday dinner at Grandfather Stevenson's with William Jennings Bryan. From prior visits, I recalled with awe how much fried chicken he could eat and I resolved to match him, piece for piece. I did, and when we reached the great Chautauqua tent for his speech, I promptly fell sound asleep at his feet, to the great discomfiture of my parents. But I still love fried chicken—and Democrats.

My father's principal interest was agriculture as I grew up. In the twenties, he was active in the fight for the McNary-Haugen Bills, and a better break for farmers. It was natural, then, that I accepted an invitation to join the staff of George N. Peek of Illinois, a Republican leader in the farmers' long struggle, and the first Administrator of the Agricultural Adjustment Act. I dropped my law practice in Chicago and moved to Washington in the summer of 1933. While I did not contribute much to the relief of the unhappy plight of the Illinois farmer, I did have an intensive course in agricultural economics and a most enlightening introduction to the perishable "special crops" on the West Coast—everything from the dates of the desert of Southern California to the apples of Washington.

With the repeal of the prohibition amendment, in December 1933, I was "loaned" to an agency called the Federal Alcohol Control Administration, hastily improvised to regulate all the alcoholic beverage industries until more permanent legislative controls could be devised. The FACA, as it was called, was also headed by a Republican, Joseph H. Choate, Jr., of New York. For most of a year, I labored prodigiously with the infinite problems of those industries, emancipated after fifteen years, and so heavily freighted with social interest.

Then, after almost a year and a half of the intensity of the early days of the Roosevelt administration in Washington, I returned to my law firm in Chicago in the autumn of 1934. And there I stayed, occupied with the law and my first interest, foreign affairs, until I moved again to Washington in June 1941. This time it was to join my beloved friend, Colonel Frank Knox, the Secretary of the Navy, also a Republican, as his Special Assistant and Counsel. In large part, Colonel Knox's request to join him and the confidence he reposed in me during those three relentless years of the war, until his death, in April 1944, sprang from an earlier common conviction that involvement in the war seemed inevitable. I am sure that is why he disregarded the counsels of Republican regularity and the cautious advice of lesser men, and, like Henry Stimson, accepted the call of his

President to head the Navy in an hour of peril and imperative preparedness.

From the fall of France in June of 1940, I had spent much of my time in Chicago, agitating and exhorting about the sinister threat of Hitler and fascism and for aid to the Allies. Colonel Knox's newspaper, the Chicago *Daily News*, rode gallantly to battle with the Chicago *Tribune* every day in the citadel of isolation and "America First." Finally, with the clouds gathering ever darker and the pressure gauges rising rapidly in Washington, Colonel Knox asked me to drop the public-opinion battle in Chicago and join him in the Navy Department. I did, in July of 1941, and from that day until this, repose or relaxation have never been my lot.

My duties with Secretary Knox in the rapidly expanding Navy Department were many and varied. And there was much travel, including a memorable and early journey to the South Pacific with Secretary Knox and Admiral Nimitz, a journey I can never forget because of what I saw of the enormity and the cost in heroism and treasure of our undertaking to bridge and conquer the Pacific.

In the fall of 1943, Secretary Knox "loaned" me to head an economic mission to see what should and could be done about devastated, hungry, confused Italy behind the allied armies, then painfully fighting their way up the peninsula.

I think it was in Naples on a wet, cold night in that ugly winter that I naively asked Ernie Pyle if the G.I.s up at the front were much interested in the soldier-vote legislation I had just been working on in Washington. He looked at me incredulously. "No," he said, "I don't think so, but I can tell you what they *are* thinking about. They're thinking about a dry spot where they can place their bottoms and wring out their socks." Later, I went up there in the mud and blood of the Liri Valley and saw for myself. He was right.

Somewhere, there in Italy, I think, I read about a public-opinion poll which reported that some seven out of ten American parents disapproved their sons going into politics or public service, or something like that. From what I had already seen of the war at home, in the Pacific, in the Mediterranean and from what I was still to see in Europe, I've often thought of that little morsel of news: fight, suffer, die, squander our substance, yes; but work in peacetime for the things we die for in war, no! There seemed to me something curiously inconsistent about the glorious, eager, uncomplaining sacrifices of war for the security of our homeland and its cherished institutions, and the active distaste of so many respectable people for peacetime participation in the politics and service of that homeland and its institutions. Die for them—yes; work for them—no. Small wonder, I thought, that our "politics" is no better, and great wonder that it is as good as it is. It seems to me sad that "politics" and "politician" are so often epithets and words of disrespect and contempt, and not without justification, in the land of Jefferson and in a government by the governed.

But it is an old story. Dickens and everyone else has had something to say about it. . . . Of one thing I am sure, however; the regeneration of our politics and public life at our maturity and zenith is moving apace and in the right direction. But there is a long way to go.

A year later, in the autumn of 1944, I was in England and along the Western Front in France and Belgium on an Air Force job. Like so much of "my war" there was little time to think, to meditate on it all. I was always in a hurry. I guess I've always been in a hurry, which probably does not distinguish me much from most of my fellow Americans! Yet standing one day—wet and cold—in Eschweiler, a battered little town on the German frontier, I thought of Italy, just a year before, wet, cold and bloody too, of the South Pacific the year before that, hot, steaming and bloody, of North Africa, West Africa, the Caribbean, and all the places I had been, all the things I had seen, like the soldiers there in Eschweiler, moving up to the lines, and the ambulances moving back. I thought of the ghastly burns I had seen long before on those "Pearl Harbor boys" in the rows of white beds in California. I thought, too, of how the desperately wounded little Japanese prisoners had struggled to sit up and bow in a stinking, suffocating hospital hut in a coconut grove on the other side of the war-wrenched globe.

Was this the everlasting destiny of man, indicted for his stupidity and sin, convicted, sentenced forever to kill or be killed? No, it would end soon. "The weather is too bad for tactical flying," the officer was saying, "but the Eighth Air Force will be over tonight to flatten some more of Berlin, I suppose." And beyond, I thought, was the Russian juggernaut pounding, grinding toward us; the noose was tightening—yes, it would be over soon; and then we must start on something better; pick up where Wilson left off, with a broken heart and a broken body, and push on to end this ugly business before it ends us all; what was it Wilson said in his sorrow with the prescience of revelation: "For I can tell you, my fellow citizens, I can predict with absolute certainty that within another generation there will be another world war if the nations of the world do not concert the method by which to prevent it."

It wasn't a long reverie, just a moment, there near the command post, in December 1944, before the big push across the Rhine. The next day we started back across Belgium by automobile on the way to London. That night the Battle of the Bulge commenced, and the last Nazi convulsion was smothered in the forest of Ardennes which had been so still and beautiful in the soft fresh snow.

Back home, when my friends, Edward Stettinius, then Secretary of State, and Archibald MacLeish, Assistant Secretary, asked me to come into the State Department to help out "for a few months" with the United Nations planning, I accepted.

They used to say that if you worked in wartime Washington, you would get one of three things: galloping frustration, ulcers or a sense of humor. I guess I got them all and I also got a great education in war, the world, our government and my fellow man under every sort of trial and tension, from Congressional investigations to that shattering evening in the Secretary of the Navy's office while the news from Pearl Harbor was coming in. But I think my most intensive postgraduate education commenced that day I entered the State Departent as Assistant to the Secretary, late in February 1945.

Instead of a few months, I stayed a year. Instead of going back to Chicago after the San Francisco Conference as I had planned, I went to London as deputy to Stettinius on the Preparatory Commission of the U.N. When he shortly fell ill and had to return to the United States, I succeeded him as chief of our delegation and lived in London for almost six months. It was the most exacting, interesting and, in many ways, the most important interval of my life. After almost four years of preoccupation with war, the satisfaction of having a part in the organized search for the conditions and mechanics of peace completed my circle.

After our work in London was done, Secretary of State Byrnes asked me to go to Argentina or Brazil as our Ambassador, but I went back to Chicago, my family and law firm, in March 1946. President Truman asked me to serve on our delegation to the United Nations that fall and I spent three more sleepless months at the General Assembly in New York. He appointed me again in 1947, and for another three months I worked with our delegation in New York, an interval which confirmed with finality misgivings I had sorrowfully expressed early in 1946 about Russian intentions and our hopes for future tranquility.

When I returned to Chicago in December 1947, some of the Democratic leaders asked me to run for Governor. This was a new departure indeed. I had never run for any office, had never wanted any, had never been active in city or state politics and knew almost none of the party leaders in Chicago or downstate. Moreover, 1948 didn't look like a very good year for Democrats anywhere, let alone in Illinois where only three had been elected Governor in ninety years. But I accepted. Why? I don't know exactly; perhaps it was because of Father and Grandfather Stevenson and Great-Grandfather Fell who had all served Illinois; perhaps it was restlessness about settling down again after eight feverish years of war and peace; perhaps it was the encouragement of some determined friends . . . and perhaps the public-opinion poll I saw in Italy had something to do with it.

Anyway, I did it. I worked at it day and night, from January to November, and was elected by the largest majority in the state's history. There followed four years of toil in Springfield, more rewarding and more satisfying than I dreamed possible. The governorship of a great state is an intensive education in politics, people and public administration that has few counterparts in American public life. There I discovered that in a political job there are usually two ways to do things: the politically expedient way or the right way. Sometimes they do not coincide but, in the long run, the right way is the best politics.

In front of the governor's mansion, Springfield, Illinois.

II

THE GOVERNOR

When Adlai Stevenson returned to Chicago from his duties with the fledgling United Nations in December 1947, friends and supporters persuaded him to seek the nomination for United States Senator from Illinois. But Colonel Jacob Arvey, leader of the Democratic organization in Illinois, decided that Paul Douglas was his choice for that job, and he offered Stevenson, instead, the nomination for governor. Stevenson hesitated, reluctant to seek a job that would so utterly separate him from any role in foreign affairs, but at length he accepted and was duly nominated. At the time he did not seem likely to win. His name was unknown in the state and, furthermore, Illinois had elected only three Democrats as governor since the Civil War.

Stevenson campaigned on the grounds that he had no political obligations to anyone and that he intended to bring honesty back into the state government, as well as modernize it. In the middle of the campaign a series of accidents brought to light a deep-running system of graft and corruption in the incumbent Republican's administration, and when the votes were counted on November 5, Adlai Stevenson had carried the state by the largest plurality in its history. It seems likely that his strength—revealed by a margin of 572,067 votes—was decisive for Harry Truman, who won in Illinois by a narrow edge of 33,612 votes.

Shortly after Stevenson was elected, he and his wife separated, and not long afterwards she divorced him. They had three sons: Adlai III, Borden, and John Fell. The oldest was already at college; the youngest was thirteen years old. After the divorce, Stevenson's sister, Mrs. Ernest Ives, occasionally played hostess at the governor's mansion, but essentially the governor lived an ascetic life there, entertaining infrequently and often working well into the night.

A TWO-EDGED SWORD AGAINST SUBVERSION *From Stevenson's message that accompanied his veto of the so-called Broyles Bill, which was passed in 1951 by both houses of the state legislature and then came to the governor for approval.*

I veto and withhold my approval from this bill [Senate Bill No. 102] for the following reasons:

The stated purpose of this bill is to combat the menace of world communism. That the Communist party—and all it stands for—is a danger to our republic, as real as it is sinister, is clear to all who have the slightest understanding of our democracy. No one attached to the principles of our society will debate this premise or quarrel with the objectives of this bill.

Agreed upon ends, our concern is with means. It is in the choice of methods to deal with recognized problems that we Americans, in and out of public life, so often develop differences of opinion. Our freedom to do so is a great source of strength and, if not impaired by mistakes of our own, will contribute greatly to the ultimate confusion of the enemies of freedom.

The issue with respect to means raised by this bill has two aspects. One is the question of the need for it in relation to existing weapons for the control of subversives. The other is whether this addition to our arsenal may not be a two-edged sword, more dangerous to ourselves than to our foes.

Were the latter alone involved, I should hesitate to impose my judgment upon that of the majority of the General Assembly. But it is precisely because the evil at hand has long since been identified and provided against that we here in Illinois need not now do something bad just for the sake of doing something. □

Senate Bill No. 102 makes it a felony to commit or attempt any act intended to overthrow by force the federal or state governments, or any of their political subdivisions; to advocate or teach the commission of such acts; or to have any connection with an organization devoted to such an objective. This approach parallels and duplicates criminal statutes of both the federal and state governments already in effect. Nor am I aware of complaints by any State's Attorneys throughout Illinois that our present sedition laws are insufficient.

Not only does Senate Bill No. 102 appear wholly unnecessary, but I agree with the Bar Associations that if the present sedition laws could be strengthened by expressly prohibiting the commission of acts as well as the advocacy thereof, this could best be accomplished by amending the existing laws rather than enacting new and more laws. Criminal laws, especially on subjects of vital importance, should not be confused by patchwork and duplication.

But it is in the enforcement provisions that I find this bill most objectionable. The Attorney General of Illinois is directed to appoint a Special Assistant Attorney General who must assemble and deliver to the State's Attorney of each county all information relating to subversive acts or activities within such county. The local State's Attorney then must present this matter to the Grand Jury. The Assistant Attorney General in Springfield must maintain complete records of all such information which may, with the permission of the Attorney General, be made public.

The transmission of such information and the subsequent presentation of it to the Grand Jury is mandatory under the Act—and covers in terms all information, however inconclusive or insignificant. I know of no precedent of any such interference with the normal discretion accorded to a public prosecutor. One of the important responsibilities of State's Attorneys and one of the greatest protections of the citizen is the exercise of sound judgment in sifting the many rumors, charges and counter-charges which come to State's Attorneys' attention. This is true in the operation of the criminal laws generally, and it must, of necessity, be even more true when we are dealing with criminal laws relating in large degree to the state of men's minds.

I can see nothing but grave peril to the reputation of innocent people in this perpetuation of rumors and hearsay. When we already have sedition laws prohibiting the offenses to which these provisions relate, I see more danger than safety in such radical change in the administration of criminal justice.

Other substantive provisions in the bill are intended to assure the loyalty of the employees of the state government and its political subdivisions. All agencies of government must establish procedures to ascertain that there are no reasonable

Governor Stevenson on the steps of the state capitol in Springfield, behind a statue of Stephen Douglas. The Dalmation is Stevenson's dog, King Arthur, generally known as Artie.

Stevenson in his ground-floor office at the governor's mansion.

Stevenson in his ground-floor office at the governor's mansion.

grounds to believe that any applicant for employment is committed, by act or teaching, to the overthrow of the government by force or is a member of an organization dedicated to that purpose. Thus, one who wishes to work for the state or to teach in a school must himself carry the burden of proving the absence of any reasonable grounds for belief that he is subversive or even belongs to a subversive organization. The bill does not even require that the applicant for employment know the purpose of such an organization.

Provisions as to those already employed also shift the burden of proof to the employee. With all the multitude of employing agencies throughout the state, each establishing its own rule and procedures for the enforcement of these provisions, it is easy to see what variations there might be and what possibilities for discrimination depending upon the wisdom and fairness of the particular employer.

By such provisions as these, irreparable injury to the reputation of innocent persons is more than a possibility, it is a likelihood. If this bill became law, it would be only human for employees to play safe and shirk duties which might bring upon them resentment or criticism. Public service requires independent and courageous action on matters which affect countless private interests. We cannot afford to make public employees vulnerable to malicious charges of disloyalty. So far as the employers are concerned—heads of departments and of schools and so on—the only safe policy would be timid employment practices which could only result in a lowering of the level of ability, independence and courage in our private agencies, schools and colleges.

If this bill became law, it would be only human for employees to play safe and shirk duties which might bring upon them resentment or criticism. Public service requires independent and courageous action on matters which affect countless private interests. We cannot afford .to make public employees vulnerable to malicious charges of disloyalty. So far as the employers are concerned—heads· of departments.and of schools and so on—the only safe policy would be timid employment practices which could only result in a lowering of the level of ability, independence and courage in our public agencies, schools and colleges.

Lastly, the bill provides that a candidate for public office, other than offices for which an oath is prescribed by the Constitution, shall file an affidavit that he is not a subversive person. The Attorney General informs me that, despite the exception made, this requirement is of dubious constitutionality.

Does anyone seriously think that a real traitor will hesitate to sign a loyalty oath? Of course not. Really dangerous subversives and saboteurs will be caught by careful, constant, professional investigation, not by pieces of paper.

The whole notion of loyalty inquisitions is a natural characteristic of the police state, not of democracy. Knowing his rule rests upon compulsion rather than consent, the dictator must always assume the disloyalty not of a few but of many, and guard against it by continual inquisition and "liquidation" of the unreliable. The history of Soviet Russia is a modern example of this ancient practice. The democratic state, on the other hand, is based on the consent of its members. The

vast majority of our people are intensely loyal, as they have amply demonstrated. To question, even by implication, the loyalty and devotion of a large group of citizens is to create an atmosphere of suspicion and distrust which is neither justified, healthy nor consistent with our traditions.

Legislation of this type, in Illinois and elsewhere, is the direct result of the menacing gains of communism in Europe and Asia. But it would be unrealistic, if not naive, to assume that such legislation would be effective in combatting Communist treachery in America. Such state laws have nowhere uncovered a single case of subversive disloyalty.

Basically, the effect of this legislation, then, will be less the detection of subversives and more the intimidation of honest citizens. But we cannot suppress thought and expression and preserve the freedoms guaranteed by the Bill of Rights. That is our dilemma. In time of danger we seek to protect ourselves from sedition, but in doing so we imperil the very freedoms we seek to protect, just as we did in the evil atmosphere of the alien and sedition laws of John Adams' administration and just as Britain did during the Napoleonic era. To resolve the dilemma we will all agree that in the last analysis the republic must be protected at all costs, or there will be no freedoms to preserve or even regain. But if better means of protection already exist, then surely we should not further imperil the strength of freedom in search of illusory safety.

We must fight traitors with laws. We already have the laws. We must fight falsehood and evil ideas with truth and better ideas. We have them in plenty. But we must not confuse the two. Laws infringing our rights and intimidating unoffending persons without enlarging our security will neither catch subversives nor win converts to our better ideas.

Finally, the states are not, in my judgment, equipped to deal with the threat of the world Communist movement which inspired this bill. Communism threatens us because it threatens world peace. The great problems with which it confronts us are problems of foreign relations and national defense. Our Constitution wisely leaves the solution of such matters to the national government.

In conclusion, while I respect the motives and patriotism of the proponents of this bill, I think there is in it more of danger to the liberties we seek to protect than of security for the republic. It reverses our traditional concept of justice by placing upon the accused the burden of proving himself innocent. It makes felons of persons who may be guilty more of bad judgment than anything else. It jeopardizes the freedom of sincere and honest citizens in an attempt to catch and punish subversives. It is unnecessary and redundant. □

I know that to veto this bill in this period of grave anxiety will be unpopular with many. But I must, in good conscience, protest against any unnecessary suppression of our ancient rights as free men. Moreover, we will win the contest of ideas that afflicts the world not by suppressing these rights, but by their triumph. We must not burn down the house to kill the rats.

FAREWELL TO THE CITIZENS OF ILLINOIS *From Stevenson's farewell report as governor, at Springfield, the state capital, January 8, 1953.*

I wish I could review here everything that has been done or attempted since 1949 to improve our state government. I should like to review these crowded years, department by department—from hunting and fishing and wildlife conservation to insurance regulation—our successes and our failures, our triumphs and defeats, what I've learned that's so and what I've learned that isn't so. I would like to talk to you about politics and patronage, about law enforcement, gambling, corruption, about human beings, the good and the evil, and all the things that have made these four relentless years here in Springfield the best in my life.

You would understand better then why I am so grateful for the opportunity you, the people, gave me and why I wanted so desperately to continue here in Springfield. But my party asked me to run for President and, after preaching the gospel of public service so long, I didn't see how I could consistently decline. The consequences are familiar to you, and acutely familiar to me now, on the eve of my return to private life!

But all that is past, and it is with the future that I shall deal. I have listed some ten major future goals for the state. They contain no sensations. In the past four years, we have instituted extensive legislative and administrative changes. I am happy to say that most of the ambitious original objectives I had four years ago have now been accomplished in whole or in part. What follows are the principal things that remain to be done as I see it:

1. Foremost is the highway program. It must be completed as soon as possible. □

2. The urgent needs of the public schools must continue to be recognized. The schools represent our greatest asset. □

3. We must extend the gains in welfare services and administration. □

4. The state penal system must be re-examined. □

5. Law enforcement must be tightened. □

6. Efforts to modernize the state constitution and the state government should continue. □

7. Better mine safety and labor laws are needed. □

8. The civil rights of all citizens must be steadfastly protected. □

9. A single board for higher education should be created. □

10. The merit idea in personnel policies and recruitment should be extended.

The efficient functioning and integrity of government depend upon attracting to public life honest, competent, loyal men and women. Of all the things I have tried to do, nothing is more important than the progress we have made in bringing to and retaining in the state service capable men and women without regard to politics. □

This then is my report on the condition of the state:

Our financial position is strong, significant changes have been initiated in state government organization, the people are getting the kind of public service at the state level which they are entitled to expect. Our regulatory agencies have

The governor going up to bed, but not without a folder of work still to be done.

acquired a reputation for objectivity, competence and freedom from influence. Public employees expect to do, and do, a full day's work for a day's pay.

There has, in short, been a brightening of the tradition of state government in Illinois. With the type of public responsibility we have sought to achieve, with a fearless facing of the people's needs and demands, we can make effective state government a reality, and thus avoid those failures of performance which so often cause public functions to move up the ladder to Washington.

Government—local, state and federal—is not something separate and apart; if it is to be good, it must share the attitudes and the competence of the best in our society as a whole. Both business and government are gainers when the best among us from private life will make the sacrifice, if need be, to fill vital public positions.

Illinois, where my family have lived and prospered for a century and a quarter, means a great deal to me, and I am humbly thankful for the opportunity that has been mine to serve it. I leave my high office content in one respect—that I have given to it the best that was in me. It has been a richly rewarding experience, and the satisfactions have far outweighed the disappointments.

To the people of Illinois who have honored me so generously, and to the associates in this great undertaking whose friendship and loyalty have meant so much to me, I shall be eternally grateful.

And now, with a full heart, I bid you all good-bye.

The reluctant candidate at his farm in Libertyville, Illinois, a few weeks before the Democratic convention.

The reluctant candidate at his farm in Libertyville, Illinois, a few weeks before the Democratic convention.

III

THE FIRST PRESIDENTIAL CAMPAIGN

In January 1952 Adlai Stevenson filed for renomination for the governorship of Illinois. Late that same month in Washington, President Truman told him privately that he did not intend to run for reelection, and that in his opinion Stevenson was the strongest candidate the Democrats could choose. Essentially, it was an offer of the nomination. Stevenson flabbergasted the President by refusing, both then and in a second conversation two months later. When Truman publicly announced his retirement in late March, the pressure on Stevenson to say that he would run became enormous. But he stoutly held to his position that he was a candidate for the governorship of Illinois, not the Presidency. Mail and newspaper correspondents flooded his office, but he stood firm until the Democratic convention itself. His welcoming address as governor of the host state was inspiring; the tide in his favor rose. Finally Stevenson yielded. The nomination was his on the third ballot, and next day Senator John Sparkman of Alabama was chosen as the Vice-Presidential candidate. Stevenson went back to Springfield to gather his wits and to organize a major campaign from scratch.

A CANDIDATE FOR GOVERNOR *An announcement made April 15, 1952, at Springfield, Illinois.*

I have been urged to announce my candidacy for the Democratic nomination for President, but I am a candidate for Governor of Illinois and I cannot run for two offices at the same time. Moreover, my duties as Governor do not presently afford the time to campaign for the nomination, even if I wanted it.

Others have asked me merely to say that I would accept a nomination which I did not seek. To state my position now on a prospect so remote in time and probability seems to me a little presumptuous. But I would rather presume than embarrass or mislead.

In these somber years the hopes of mankind dwell with the President of the United States. From such responsibility one does not shrink in fear, self-interest or humility. But great political parties, like great nations, have no indispensable man, and last January, before I was even considered for the Presidency, I announced that I would seek re-election as Governor of Illinois. Last week I was nominated in the Democratic primary. It is the highest office within the gift of the citizens of Illinois, and its power for good or ill over their lives is correspondingly great. No one should lightly aspire to it or lightly abandon the quest once begun.

Hence, I have repeatedly said that I was a candidate for Governor of Illinois and had no other ambition. To this I must now add that, in view of my prior commitment to run for Governor and my desire and the desire of many who have given me their help and confidence in our unfinished work in Illinois, I could not accept the nomination for any other office this summer.

Better state government is the only sound foundation for our federal system, and I am proud and content to stand on my commitment to ask the people of Illinois to allow me to continue for another four years in my present post.

I cannot hope that my situation will be universally understood or my conclusions unanimously approved.

I can hope that friends with larger ambitions for me will not think ill of me. They have paid me the greatest compliment within their gift, and they have my utmost gratitude.

SPEECH OF ACCEPTANCE *From his first speech as the Democratic Presidential candidate, Chicago, July 26, 1952, at 3:00 A.M.*

I accept your nomination—and your program.

I should have preferred to hear those words uttered by a stronger, a wiser, a better man than myself. But, after listening to the President's speech, I feel better about myself!

None of you, my friends, can wholly appreciate what is in my heart. I can only hope that you may understand my words. They will be few.

I have not sought the honor you have done me. I *could* not seek it because I aspired to another office, which was the full measure of my ambition. One does not treat the highest office within the gift of the people of Illinois as an alternative or as a consolation prize.

I *would* not seek your nomination for the Presidency because the burdens of that office stagger the imagination. Its potential for good or evil, now and in the years of our lives, smothers exultation and converts vanity to prayer.

I have asked the Merciful Father—the Father of us all—to let this cup pass from me. But from such dread responsibility one does not shrink in fear, in self-interest or in false humility.

So, "If this cup may not pass from me, except I drink it, Thy will be done."

That my heart has been troubled, that I have not sought this nomination, that I could not seek it in good conscience, that I would not seek it in honest self-appraisal, is not to say that I value it the less. Rather it is that I revere the office of the Presidency of the United States.

And now, my friends, that you have made your decision, I will fight to win that office with all my heart and soul. And, with your help, I have no doubt that we will win. □

What does concern me, in common with thinking partisans of both parties, is not just winning the election, but how it is won, how well we can take advantage of this great quadrennial opportunity to debate issues sensibly and soberly. I hope and pray that we Democrats, win or lose, can campaign not as a crusade to exterminate the opposing party, as our opponents seem to prefer, but as a great opportunity to educate and elevate a people whose destiny is leadership, not alone of a rich and prosperous, contented country as in the past, but of a world in ferment.

And, my friends, more important than winning the election is governing the nation. That is the test of a political party—the acid, final test. When the tumult and the shouting die, when the bands are gone and the lights are dimmed, there is the stark reality of responsibility in an hour of history haunted with those gaunt, grim specters of strife, dissension and materialism at home, and ruthless, inscrutable and hostile power abroad.

The ordeal of the twentieth century—the bloodiest, most turbulent era of the Christian age—is far from over. Sacrifice, patience, understanding and implacable purpose may be our lot for years to come. Let's face it. Let's talk sense to the American people. Let's tell them the truth, that there are no gains without pains, that we are now on the eve of great decisions, not easy decisions, like resistance when you're attacked, but a long, patient, costly struggle which alone can assure triumph over the great enemies of man—war, poverty and tyranny—and the assaults upon human dignity which are the most grievous consequences of each.

Let's tell them that the victory to be won in the twentieth century, this portal to the Golden Age, mocks the pretensions of individual acumen and ingenuity. For it is a citadel guarded by thick walls of ignorance and of mistrust which do not fall before the trumpets' blast or the politicians' imprecations or even a general's baton. They are, my friends, walls that must be directly stormed by the hosts of courage, of morality and of vision, standing shoulder to shoulder, unafraid of ugly truth, contemptuous of lies, half truths, circuses and demagoguery.

The people are wise—wiser than the Republicans think. And the Democratic Party is the people's party, not the labor party, not the farmers' party, not the employers' party—it is the party of no one because it is the party of everyone.

That, I think, is our ancient mission. Where we have deserted it, we have failed. With your help, there will be no desertion now. Better we lose the election than mislead the people and better we lose than misgovern the people. Help me to do the job in this autumn of conflict and of campaign; help me to do the job in these years of darkness, doubt and of crisis which stretch beyond the horizon of tonight's happy vision, and we will justify our glorious past and the loyalty of silent millions who look to us for compassion, for understanding and for honest purpose. Thus we will serve our great tradition greatly.

I ask of you all you have; I will give to you all I have, even as he who came here tonight and honored me, as he has honored you—the Democratic party—by a lifetime of service and bravery that will find him an imperishable page in the history of the Republic and of the Democratic party—President Harry S. Truman.

And finally, my friends, in the staggering task you have assigned me, I shall always try "to do justly and to love mercy and to walk humbly with my God."

THE EXACTING ORDEAL *Stevenson's description of the campaign, taken from his introduction to* Major Campaign Speeches, *1952.*

At least for an inexperienced candidate, I suppose we have contrived few more exacting ordeals than a Presidential campaign. You must emerge, bright and bubbling with wisdom and well-being, every morning at eight o'clock, just in time for a charming and profound breakfast talk, shake hands with hundreds, often literally thousands, of people, make several inspiring, "newsworthy" speeches during the day, confer with political leaders along the way and with your staff all the time, write at every chance, think if possible, read mail and newspapers, talk on the telephone, talk to everybody, dictate, receive delegations, eat, with

Truman leading Stevenson to the platform at the Democratic convention to accept the party's nomination on July 26, 1952, in the early hours of the morning.

decorum—and discretion!—and ride through city after city on the back of an open car, smiling until your mouth is dehydrated by the wind, waving until the blood runs out of your arm, and then bounce gaily, confidently, masterfully into great howling halls, shaved and all made up for television with the right color shirt and tie—I always forgot—and a manuscript so defaced with chicken tracks and last-minute jottings that you couldn't follow it, even if the spotlights weren't blinding and even if the still photographers didn't shoot you in the eye every time you looked at them. (I've often wondered what happened to all those pictures!) Then all you have to do is make a great, imperishable speech, get out through the pressing crowds with a few score autographs, your clothes intact, your hands bruised, and back to the hotel—in time to see a few important people.

But the real work has just commenced—two or three, sometimes four hours of frenzied writing and editing of the next day's immortal mouthings so you can get something to the stenographers, so they can get something to the mimeograph machines, so they can get something to the reporters, so they can get something to their papers by deadline time. (And I quickly concluded that all deadlines were yesterday!) Finally sleep, sweet sleep, steals you away, unless you worry—which I do.

The next day is the same.

But I gained weight on it. And it's as tenacious as a campaign deficit! Somehow the people sustain you, the people and a constant, sobering reminder that you are asking them to entrust to you the most awesome responsibility on earth. And, too, there is mirth mingled with the misery all along the way. They shout, "Good old Ad-lie!" If you run for office and have a slightly unusual name, let me advise you either to change it before you start, or be prepared to take other people's word for it. And I shall not soon forget about the woman in the crowd in San Francisco who reached into the car to shake hands with me, and not long after discovered that she had lost her diamond ring. Nor will I forget the warm welcome I received on a whistle stop in Bethlehem and my thanks to "the people of Allentown." My only hope is that *they* forget it! Again, out West, I warmly endorsed the impressive chairman of a meeting as a candidate for Congress, only to discover that he was not running for Congress or anything else. □

How did I happen to be nominated for President when I didn't seek the nomination and didn't want it? In late December 1951, I decided after long reflection on the trials and hazards, the changes and chances of political life, to run for Governor again. There was much, much more to do in Illinois; there would be no primary contest, my chances of re-election looked very bright regardless of what happened nationally, my principal associates had agreed to stay with me for another term, the government was well organized at last, the party political tribulations of the early years had subsided, and the governorship of Illinois was a dramatic opportunity to demonstrate to all and sundry, in and out of politics, that reason will prevail—"our sandbank is bound to grow"—and that, simply stated, the best government is in fact the best politics and will pay off in public confidence and votes manyfold what it loses in patronage, profit and political organization.

So I announced for Governor again. Very shortly, articles began to appear about me as a Democratic Presidential possibility, seldom taking any note of the fact that, even if I wanted the nomination, I was already committed to run for Governor and it was too late under Illinois law for anyone else to file.

All winter and spring, people were coming to Springfield and telephoning from all over the country—newspapermen, columnists, commentators, political leaders, friends, leaders of organizations, etc., etc. The mail became a real burden. First it was exhortation to announce my candidacy and enter primaries—"fight for the nomination." To all, my explanation was the same: I was a candidate for Governor of Illinois; I was committed to run for that office and one could not run for two offices at the same time in good conscience, or treat the highest office within the gift of the people of Illinois as a consolation prize. Moreover, as the executive head of a huge business, the State of Illinois, I had little time to go around the country campaigning for an unwanted nomination for an unwanted office—an office, moreover, of such appalling difficulty and responsibility in the year of grace, 1952, that I felt no sense of adequacy.

Later, the pressure changed. It was no longer, "Will you be a candidate for the nomination?" but "Will you accept the nomination?" This was more difficult. If I said, "Yes," publicly or covertly, it would start the draft movement in earnest. If I said, "No," how would it reconcile with all my preaching about public service and politics? How could I foretell then, long before the convention, what manner of deadlock and bitterness might develop to the lasting damage of my party? And, finally, could anyone in good health and already in public life refuse the greatest honor and greatest responsibility in our political system? So I concluded to keep still and say nothing more to anyone, contenting myself with confidence that no one could, in fact, be drafted by a modern convention against his often-expressed wish. As the convention approached, that is what I told everyone, while I busied myself with the formation of committees, preparing my program and campaigning for Governor.

All this time, from January to July, I read stories speculating that I wanted to run if Senator Taft was nominated by the Republicans, but not against General Eisenhower; that I was being coy and playing hard to get; that I had promised President Truman to run if he didn't, etc., etc. And only occasionally did I see anything suggesting that I meant what I said and that another term as Governor of Illinois really was the full measure of my ambition.

I was a district delegate to the convention and, the day before it convened, I asked a caucus of the Illinois delegation not to nominate me and not to vote for me if nominated. At the opening of the convention, I made a welcoming speech as Governor of the host state, along with Martin Kennelly, the Democratic Mayor of Chicago. Something of a demonstration followed; so, after one more appearance in the hall, I stayed away on the other side of the city. Hearing that Archibald Alexander, candidate for Senator in New Jersey, or Governor Shricker of Indiana might nominate me, I called them both by phone and asked them not to. Alexander

Detroit, Michigan.

agreed, but my esteemed friend, Governor Shricker, rebelled—and a very good nominating speech he made, too!

Contrary to the impression of some, I had no understanding whatever with President Truman at any time that I was available. To set at rest still another rumor, I think my friend, Colonel Arvey, the National Committeeman from Illinois, would testify that, during those six months, I repeatedly urged him to do nothing in my behalf and repeatedly he assured me he neither had nor would, always adding that he was bedeviled with incessant pressures and inquiries.

In the circumstances that I have here attempted hastily to sketch, I was nominated and accepted the nomination at about three o'clock on the morning of July 26th. And I was delighted with the selection the following day of a very uncommon American, Senator John Sparkman of Alabama, as my running mate.

The delegates went home, most of them, I suspect, a little bewildered about the unknown, reluctant dragon they had just selected. I went to Springfield, there to contemplate the wreckage of my hopes to run for Governor and the problems of a highly inexperienced candidate for the presidency. I had limited political acquaintance, no manager, no staff, little money in the till, little press support. And I was running against General Eisenhower, a national hero for ten years, and also the inevitable accumulation of irritations and anxieties of twenty years of government in a time of profound changes—irritations and anxieties which had been vigorously, if not objectively, cultivated for a long time by Republican orators and most of the press. The best confidential polls indicated that we had no more than 35 per cent of the popular vote.

But the Republican party was badly split and the election was three months off. Like Dr. Johnson, I saw no point in expressing a consternation I didn't feel for a calamity that had not occurred. And, besides the great Democratic party and the social revolution it had wrought, I had some other assets, too; among them the prompt, warm and sincere encouragement and loyalty of all the disappointed contenders for the nomination—Senator Kefauver, Averell Harriman, Senator Kerr, Senator Russell, and my great kinsman, Alben Barkley. There was still another asset, little noted in the newspapers, which meant a great deal to me— I had literally no obligations to anyone.

I suppose, like the unsought and unwanted nomination itself, this was something new in our political history. Nor, let me add, did anyone ever ask anything of me in exchange for support or money, which, I daresay, is also something unique in presidential campaigns. □

I had nothing whatever to do with writing it, but the Democratic platform of 1952, while if not the perfection of political probity, was, I thought, a very good one indeed. I decided to adhere to it as closely as I could and, thereby, perhaps further a little the classical purpose of a periodical restatement of principles and program for the public's enlightenment.

For years I have listened to the nauseous nonsense, the pie-in-the-sky appeals to cupidity and greed, the cynical trifling with passion and prejudice and fear; the slander, fraudulent promises, and the all-things-to-all-men demagoguery that are

Listeners at a speech.

too much a part of our political campaigns. Sometimes in the deafening clamor of political salesmanship, I've thought that the people might be better served if a party purchased a half hour of radio and TV silence during which the audience would be asked to think quietly for themselves.

Politicians all applaud and support public education as democracy's great monument and cornerstone, but does the politician, the agent and spokesman of democracy, have no responsibility for public education? Government by the consent of the governed is the most difficult system of all because it depends for its success and viability on the good judgments and wise decisions of so many of us. But judgment and decision depend on information and understanding. In matters of public policy, candidates then have the greatest responsibility of all to inform truthfully, so that the people will understand and will have the tools of good judgment and wise decision.

One can argue, indeed, that candidates claiming the people's confidence have even a higher mission; honestly to help man to know, as St. Thomas Aquinas said, what he ought to believe; to know what he ought to desire; to know what he ought to do.

It is an old, old story. Call it the duty of aspirants for public office to inform, to educate, to reason with the people they seek to lead, if you please. Believing utterly in democracy and the collective reason of properly informed people, I have always thought that political campaigns for offices of great responsibility are both an opportunity and an obligation to talk sensibly and truthfully about public questions and their full implications. □

Did I talk over the people's heads? No—and that's about the only aspect of the campaign I am sure of! As I have said above, I think candidates for important offices, let alone for the Presidency of the United States in this age and day, should not treat us as fourteen-year-olds but as adults, challenging us, in the ancient tradition of all civilized people, with the assumption that we should and can and will respond to the appeal of reason and imagination.

What's more, I doubt if I could have talked over people's heads even if I had foolishly wanted to. As Franklin P. Adams said, "The average man is a great deal above the average." To be sure, many of us may be taken in now and then by professionalized emotionalism, showmanship and huckstering. And I concede that radio, television and press create the means of mass manipulation and the "sale" of political ideas and personalities. But I am not much troubled by that danger. There are too many evidences of growing political maturity and discernment in America. While the campaign of 1952 is not a good illustration because so many imponderable factors were involved, like "time for a change," Korea and my opponent's great popularity, it is safe to say that many people voted for the Democratic candidates not because we held out any comforting hope of early tax reduction, an end to the war, peace on earth and easy solutions for all our frustrations, but for exactly the opposite reason—because we did not. There were many like the woman who flattered me with her thanks for "a shot in the intellect," and the one who wrote, "I am easily swayed by emotion until I think, which I occasionally do." □

Lovingly hand-painted signs contrasted with the generally printed Republican placards.

Stevenson delighted his audiences.

Because I have profound respect for my fellow countrymen, I gave them the best I had. It can never be good enough, and my apology is that, in the fever and haste of the campaign, I could not better express what was in my heart and head.

We live in a time for greatness and greatness cannot be measured alone by the conventional yardsticks of resources, know-how and production. There are moral dimensions, too. It is the urgent duty of a political leader to lead, to touch if he can the potentials of reason, decency and humanism in man, and not only the strivings that are easier to mobilize.

The challenge of our faith and time "is the insensate worship of matter," organized in a vast international conspiracy. But the goal of life is more than material advance; it is now, and through all eternity, the triumph of spirit over matter, of love and liberty over force and violence.

In a world where masses of people at all levels of degradation and elevation are going to decide their own destiny, more and more, in a world where words like "freedom" and "justice" are meaningless to many, we are struggling to *meet* grievous assault by better satisfying the basic material needs of man. But we shall *master* the assault only by better satisfying the basic spiritual needs of man. These are hungers, too, and we alone, those of us around the globe who are free to follow the great teachers, free to believe and free to speak, are the only ones who can. For communism knows no God, and cannot satisfy the hungry heart.

To find the true balance between security and freedom, between initiative and anarchy, between tolerance and conformity, to organize vast patience and understanding for the peaceful resolution of our conflicts, to communicate the material and spiritual goals of life by the example of a superior system of self-management and self-discipline, these are the tasks of democratic statesmanship in our tense times. And these are tasks for adults, not children, for reason, not emotion, for faith, not fear.

We lost the election; we were soundly defeated. But if I talked sense, if I succeeded in expressing my ideas as I set out to do, if I educated and elevated any of us, then I am richly rewarded.

AMERICA AND ASIA *From a speech delivered in San Francisco, September 9, 1952.*

America is threatened as never before. The question history asks and which we must answer is whether the idea of individualism—the idea of personal freedom for you and me—is equal to the idea of collectivism—the idea of personal subordination to the state; whether the idea of maximum personal liberty is equal to the idea of maximum personal discipline.

This ancient contest between freedom and despotism, which is renewed in every generation, is acute in ours. And the most important single event, it seems to me, in our history is that it is our turn to be freedom's shield and sanctuary.

I don't think that war is an inevitable part of this contest. Even the most ambitious and ruthless men do not deliberately invite destruction of the basis of

their power. They can throw the iron dice, but they know they cannot foretell the fortunes of war.

We who are free must have great strength in order that weakness will not tempt the ambitious. And the measure of the strength we must have is not what we would like to afford but what the adversary compels us to afford.

With 85 per cent of our budget allocated to defense, it is the Soviet Union which now fixes the level of our defense expenditures and thus of our tax rates. The only way to emancipate ourselves from this foreign control, and to cut taxes substantially, is first to develop our strength and then to find the means of ending the armaments race.

And here let me say something to those abroad who may mistake our present wrangling for weakness. We have always had differences of opinion which have produced all sorts of noises and confusion—especially in campaign years! But it is the kind of noise that, to the inner ear, is the sweet music of free institutions. It is the kind of noise that has produced the harmony of firm purpose whenever our people have been put to the test. The costliest blunders have been made by dictators who did not quite understand the workings of real democracy and who mistook diversity for disunity.

No one can predict, and it would be foolish to try to predict, how and when the peaceful purpose of our power will succeed in creating a just and durable peace. But are our efforts conditional upon assurance of prompt success? To answer "yes" would be to accept the certainty of eventual defeat. □

Across the continent of Asia, more than a billion of the world's peoples are churning in one of history's greatest upheavals. All the struggles of man over the centuries—economic, political, spiritual—have come together in Asia and now seem to be reaching a climax.

The causes behind that upheaval are many and varied. But there is nothing complicated about what the people want. They want a decent living—and they want freedom.

The word used most frequently by Asians to describe their aspirations is nationalism.

Nationalism to Asians means a chance to stand on their own feet, a chance to govern themselves, a chance to develop their resources for their own welfare, and a chance to prove that the color of their skins has nothing to do with their right to walk with self-respect among their fellow men in the world. Nationalism to them means the end of a legalized inferiority. It means pride, spirit, faith.

This type of nationalism is not inconsistent with closer co-operation among nations nor with the need for an enforceable peace. The Asians actually regard freedom and national independence as the doorway to international order—just as we do.

Russia's interest in Asia is nothing new.

The expansionist aims of Russia did not change with the passing of the Czars. But today the steel glove of a revolutionary ideology covers the heavy hand of imperialist expansion.

The strategy of communism in Asia is to pose as the champion—the only champion—of the Asian peoples. Communism has not created the cause or the forces behind Asia's vast upheaval. It is attempting to give direction to those forces. It seeks to impose its own label on the multiple revolutions going on in Asia today by identifying itself with the deeply felt needs and hopes of the Asian peoples.

There's an important difference, it seems to me, between communism as we view it and communism as some of the Asian peoples view it. When we think of communism, we think of what we are going to lose. When many of the Asiatics think of communism, they think of what they are going to gain—especially if they believe that they have nothing to lose.

It's important that we know these things and think about them, for we shall never be able to cope with communism unless we understand the emotional basis of its appeal.

The communists have failed to incite the workers to revolution in Western Europe. They have failed to turn the Western Allies one against the other.

But the communists may well believe that, in the aspirations and the grievances of the East, they now have the key to world power. They hope, and perhaps even expect, that the West cannot rise to the challenge in the East.

Furthermore, they may not feel the same need for quick and tidy solutions that is felt in certain quarters in our own country. They may believe that they can afford to have a patience equal to the stakes involved.

And the stakes are nothing less than an overwhelming preponderance of power—for with Asia under control, they could turn with new energy and vast new resources in an effort to win a bloodless victory in a weakened, frightened Europe.

These communist expectations define the dimensions of the threat we face in Asia and of the tasks which lie ahead for us—tasks which can be met only by disciplined, resourceful, imaginative and reasoned effort. It is an effort which has two parts: defense and development.

There is active fighting, as we all know, in Maylaya and in Indo-China. Have we given fitting recognition to the hard, bitter and prolonged efforts of the British, the French, the native Maylayan and Indo-Chinese forces? These efforts have involved heavy loss of life and great material costs.

What will the defensive task require of us in these areas, and in the Philippines, Formosa, Japan and Korea? What contributions, what commitments to security in this area should we make and can we make to the emerging system of Pacific defense?

These are some of the questions, the hard, ugly questions we must face before disaster, not afterward. This is no time, it seems to me, to kid ourselves with press agents' platitudes.

In Korea, we took a long step toward building a security system in Asia. As an American, I am proud that we had the courage to resist that ruthless, cynical aggression; and I am equally proud that we have had the fortitude to refuse to

47

risk extension of that war despite extreme communist provocations and reckless Republican criticisms.

Whatever unscrupulous politicians may say to exploit grief, tragedy and discontent for votes, history will never record that Korea was a "useless" war, unless today's heroism is watered with tomorrow's cowardice.

On other occasions I have spoken and written much about the solid accomplishments which the Korean war has made possible. Tonight let me say only this:

I believe we may in time look back at Korea as a major turning point in history—a turning point which led, not to another terrible war but to the first historic demonstration that an effective system of collective security *is* possible.

Having failed to defeat us on the field of battle, the enemy there now seeks to defeat us by prolonging the negotiations and by exhausting our patience.

But some men in this country seem to think that if definitive victory cannot be won, we should either take reckless military action or give the whole thing up. Such advice plays into the enemy's hands. The contest with tyranny is not a hundred-yard dash—it is a test of endurance.

This defensive effort in Korea and elsewhere in Asia is building a shield behind which we have the opportunity to assist in the other great task—the task of development.

Listening to the debate over China this past year, I had the distinct impression at times that the very Congressmen whose vocal cords were most active in the cause of isolation and against foreign entanglements were the same ones who were now talking as if they had wanted us to take part in a civil war in China.

The time to stop a revolution is at the beginning, not the end. But I don't recall any pleas from these critics for help for Sun Yat-sen and Chinese democracy back in the twenties. Nor did I hear them demanding intervention by the United States in the mid-thirties when civil war with the Communists broke out. Indeed it was not until quite recently, when the Chinese wars were about over, that there was even an audible whisper that we help fight a hindsight war, that we should have given more help to China than we did.

It would seem to me, my friends, that the Republican critics could better demonstrate the good faith of their concern for Asia by doing something about India and Pakistan today rather than talking about China yesterday. I don't think that tearful and interminable post-mortems about China will save any souls for democracy in the rest of Asia, the Near East and in Africa.

India is not caught up in civil strife. It can be helped in a way that is natural to us and best for it, help in the ways of peace and of social progress. India has to grow more food. It has to restore its land. It needs new resources of power. In short, it needs a democratic helping hand in the development programs it has already charted for itself.

The same is true of many other countries.

It is help of this kind that we can provide by sending agricultural experts, engineers and other trained people to these countries, and through programs of assistance to economic development.

By working with each country to expand the production of goods which are needed by other countries in the region, a self-generating and self-financing cycle of trade and development can be initiated, which will reduce and can eventually eliminate the need for American aid. At the same time, we can enlarge our export markets and develop new sources of the products we need to import.

Land reform is, of course, fundamental to the problem of Asia. But in these ways and by this kind of friendly advice and counsel we can help to guide this economic development in ways which will give powerful support to democratic political institutions.

These programs are in accordance, it seems to me, with our best traditions. And I want to assure our friends in Asia that America will never seek to dominate their political and their economic development. We will not try to make their societies over in the image of our own. On the contrary, we respect the integrity of their institutions and the rich values of their cultures. We expect to learn as well as to teach.

These programs are primarily concerned with the material needs and wants of individual men and women. Yet we do not make the mistake of believing that the answer to communist materialism is a different brand of materialism.

The answer to communism is, in the old-fashioned phrase, good works—good works inspired by love and dedicated to the whole man. The answer to the in-humanity of communism is humane respect for the individual. And the men and women of Asia desire not only to rise from wretchedness of the body but from abasement of the spirit as well.

In other words, we must strive for a harmony of means and of ends in our relations with Asia—and indeed with the rest of the world. The means of our co-operation are primarily material.

If we believe the communist threat to Asia is dangerous to us, then it is in our own self-interest to help them defend and develop, adjusting our policies to the constantly changing circumstances in a world of accelerating change. But we must not, in our necessary concern for the urgent tasks of defense and develop-ment, permit the means to obscure the end. That end is the widening and the deepening of freedom and of respect for the dignity and the worth of man.

Some may say to you that this is visionary stuff. To this I reply that history has shown again and again that the self-styled realists are the real visionaries—for their eyes are fixed on a past that cannot be recaptured. It was Woodrow Wilson, with his dream of the League of Nations, who was the truly practical man—not the Old Guard who fought him to the death. And in the fateful summer of 1940, it was the vision of a Churchill that saw beyond Dunkerque to victory.

I say that America has been called to greatness. The summons of the twentieth century is a summons to our vision, to our humanity, to our practicality. If these provide the common purpose of America and Asia, of our joint enterprise, of our progress together, we need have no fear for the future. Because it will belong to free men.

AT THE POLL *Governor Stevenson's encounter with a band of children at the place where he cast his vote on November 4, 1952.*

I would like to ask all of you children to indicate, by holding up your hands, how many of you would like to be Governor of Illinois, the way I am. [*Show of hands.*] Well, that is almost unanimous.

Now I would like to ask all the Governors if they would like to be one of you kids. [*Whereupon Stevenson cheered.*]

I don't know whether you understand what is going on here this morning very well. I am not sure I do myself! But what you see here is something that does not happen everywhere in the world. Here are a lot of your parents and your neighbors going over to the schoolhouse there to cast their vote. That means they are deciding for themselves who is going to lead them—who is going to be their leader. You understand that? They are going to decide over there who will be their officers and who runs their government, all the way from the county up to the United States.

In other words, what that means is that we decide who governs us. It is not everybody in the world who can do that. These are the things you read about in the history books, that your ancestors have been struggling for for generations —not only to get the right to govern themselves, but to keep it.

Anyway, I think you are going to remember today for one thing only, that you got a half day off from school. I am sure I have enjoyed this as much as you have, and I would like to spend the recess this morning playing with you in the school yard. But I don't know what we would play. What would we play? [*Shouts: "Baseball, football."*]

The same old fight between the cattlemen and the sheepmen. Wouldn't anybody like to have a little mock game of politics? [*A little boy: "We don't like mud fights."*]

Well, I never saw a kid who didn't like a mud fight!

You are very good to let me talk to you this morning. What I hope, as time goes on and you go further along in school, is that you will study more and more about what you have seen here this morning—this business of voting—why we vote and what we vote for. The more you study about it, the more precious it will become to you. The more you do it, the better and more intelligently you will vote, and the better government you will have. Does everybody understand that? [*Chorus of yeas.*] One of the highest degrees of intelligence in the whole United States is political intelligence.

Good-bye, kids. I hope you will all come over and see me on St. Mary's Road, but I am not over there very often any more. Good-bye. [*Chorus of "Good-bye, Governor."*]

The governor casting his ballot, November 4, 1952.

The governor casting his ballot, November 4, 1952.

CONCESSION TO EISENHOWER *Stevenson's statement to his supporters in Springfield, Illinois, just before 1:00 A.M. on November 5, 1952.*

I have a statement that I should like to make. If I may, I shall read it to you.

My fellow citizens have made their choice and have selected General Eisenhower and the Republican party as the instruments of their will for the next four years.

The people have rendered their verdict and I gladly accept it.

General Eisenhower has been a great leader in war. He has been a vigorous and valiant opponent in the campaign. These qualities will now be dedicated to leading us all through the next four years.

It is traditionally American to fight hard before an election. It is equally traditional to close ranks as soon as the people have spoken.

From the depths of my heart, I thank all of my party and all of those Independents and Republicans who supported Senator Sparkman and me.

That which unites us as American citizens is far greater than that which divides us as political parties.

I urge you all to give General Eisenhower the support he will need to carry out the great tasks that lie before him.

I pledge him mine.

We vote as many, but we pray as one. With a united people, with faith in democracy, with common concern for others less fortunate around the globe, we shall move forward with God's guidance toward the time when His children shall grow in freedom and dignity in a world at peace.

I have sent the following telegram to General Eisenhower at the Commodore Hotel in New York: "The people have made their choice and I congratulate you. That you may be the servant and guardian of peace and make the vale of trouble a door of hope is my earnest prayer. Best wishes, Adlai E. Stevenson."

Someone asked me, as I came in, down on the street, how I felt, and I was reminded of a story that a fellow-townsman of ours used to tell—Abraham Lincoln. They asked him how he felt once after an unsuccessful election. He said he felt like a little boy who had stubbed his toe in the dark. He said that he was too old to cry, but it hurt too much to laugh.

Close to midnight on election night, at the governor's mansion in Springfield. The radio was announcing an Eisenhower landslide.

IV

LEADER OF THE OPPOSITION

In January 1953 Stevenson finished his term as governor, and formally he was out of a job. But instead of retiring into relative obscurity in the accepted manner of defeated candidates, he chose to lead an intelligent and outspoken opposition and to speak out on policy whenever he disagreed seriously with Eisenhower's administration.

Stevenson's name was frequently in the news. Scarcely a month after he left Springfield, he set out with several associates on a six-month trip that took him to thirty countries around the world. He wrote articles during his travels and spoke at length about what he had learned when he came home. While he was away, his 1952 campaign speeches were published in book form and had an excellent sale. In March 1954 Stevenson delivered the honored series of Godkin lectures at Harvard (later published as a book under the title Call to Greatness*), in which he discussed the world-wide crisis rising up in the wake of retreating empires in Asia and Africa, and suggested what America's role should be in that crisis.*

Throughout the time between 1952 and 1956, Stevenson's opposition to the Eisenhower administration became firmer. He particularly attacked its foreign policy and its tolerance of McCarthyism. This criticism reached a peak during the 1954 Congressional elections. Stevenson campaigned at length for Democrats in a number of states, and when the Democrats won a majority in both houses, in spite of the popular President's endorsement of Republican candidates, it was in part a tribute to Stevenson himself. For a time after that Stevenson slowed down his public schedule, feeling he had discharged his immediate duty to his party. But he never stopped speaking altogether, and by 1955 the next campaign had really begun.

A FUNNY THING HAPPENED *A speech to the members of the Gridiron Club in Washington, D.C., December 13, 1952.*

A funny thing happened to me on the way to the White House!

The fact was, of course, that the General was so far ahead we never even saw him. I was happy to hear that I had even placed second. But no one will say, I trust, that I snatched defeat from the jaws of victory.

Which reminds me that four years ago, occupying the seat I occupy tonight, was another great Governor [Thomas E. Dewey of New York]—excuse me, the Governor of another great state—some say the second greatest state in the Union. What just happened to me had just happened to him. In fact, it had just happened to him for the second time.

But did he despair? He did not. He said to himself—if I may take a newspaper man's license and tell you what a man says to himself—he said: "If I cannot be President myself, I can at least make somebody else President." Which, blast his merry heart, he proceeded to do. Look at him now. He's as contented as the cat that swallowed the canary, or should I say, the cabinet.

At that Gridiron dinner just four years ago, the newly elected Governor of Illinois sat down there with you common people—which reminds me that I rather enjoy talking over your heads—at last! I was happy and carefree and had nothing to worry about; nothing except the organization of a new administration to clean up the state of Illinois after the long years of the usual Republican misrule.

I, a Democrat, had just been elected Governor by the largest majority ever received in Republican Illinois. And here I am, four years later, just defeated by the largest majority ever received in Democratic America.

I had not planned it that way. I had wished to continue as Governor of Illinois, there to erect a shining temple of administrative purity and political probity. But the gods decreed otherwise—after meeting in the Chicago stockyards. Mindful of the Chinese maiden's philosophical acceptance of unwanted and aggressive attentions, I concluded to accept my fate gallantly and joyfully.

Now I content myself that it is all for the best. After all, didn't Socrates say that the duty of a man of real principle is to stay out of politics? So you see I'm delighted that the sovereign people have put an even higher value on my principles than I did.

I am happy that almost 27,000,000 voted for me. I was a little baffled by the emergence of that word "egghead" to describe some of my supporters. It seems to have been first used to describe the more intelligentsiac members of that lunatic fringe who thought I was going to win. I am happy to note you have refrained from saying of the eggheads that the yolk was on them.

I enjoyed the campaign—in spots. There were times, I confess, when I was afraid I wouldn't die, times when I felt I wouldn't do it to a dog. Let me add, by the way, that, like every red-blooded American patriot, I own a dog. It was not a campaign contribution. And I think the General would say to me that there are times when he wishes he was in my shoes—you see I had them fixed.

As to my future: Well, there are those like the man who changed the sign on his car after the election from "Switched to Stevenson" to "Switched, Bothered and Bewildered," who feel that I should devote my classic talents to the welfare of mankind by frequent talking.

Then there is another smaller group who insist that God and/or the election has appointed me the scourge of the Republican party. And, finally, there is the much smaller group that feels that it is not wholly unworthy or improper to earn a living. My sons are numbered in the latter group.

But despite anything that you may have read or written, there are some plans of action that I have definitely rejected. I have declined an invitation to become president of the National Association of Gagwriters. And I will not go into vaudeville. It is equally definite that I will not become manager of the Washington Senators—I mean Clark Griffith's, not Mr. Taft's.

I have great faith in the people. As to their wisdom, well, Coca-Cola still outsells champagne. They may make mistakes. They do sometimes. But, given time, they correct their mistakes—at two- or four-year intervals.

I have faith in the people—and in their chosen leaders: men of high purpose, good will and humble hearts; men quite prepared to stand aside when the time comes and allow even more humble men to take over.

THE OPPOSITION PARTY *From a speech given in Los Angeles, February 26, 1953.*

While we may be a defeated party, we are not a beaten party. We are not a beaten party for many reasons, and the most important is that we have been honest with the people. We made no effort to sugar-coat bitter problems so that they would be easier to swallow. We told the truth; we spoke our minds. And we emerged from the campaign with more good will in the bank than any other defeated party in recent history. I am confident that if we continue to be forthright with the American people, our bank account of respect will continue to grow.

We must, therefore, be honest with the people by supporting the new administration when we believe it to be serving the national interest. □

Forty years ago, the Democratic party was just assuming power after a long period out of office. In that moment of triumph, Woodrow Wilson said this in his first inaugural address: "The success of a party means little except when the nation is using that party for a large and definite purpose." Now that is a chastening statement of principle which our Republican friends would do well to bear in mind. And each of us as citizens, owing as we do our first allegiance to the purposes of our country rather than to those of our party, should be careful never to obstruct the one in order to advance the other.

Wilson's sober appraisal of the significance of party victory can be validly applied to our own present situation. A political party which cannot in defeat make itself an effective instrument of larger national purposes is without significance in the future political life of the country; and, sooner rather than later, it will be so marked by the people to whom it must look for the return of trust and confidence and victory.

One of the most challenging aspects of this job is that it seems never to have been done well in the past. Latterly, in twenty years of opposition, the Republican party never distinguished itself except by the shrill vehemence of its criticism of the imperative adjustments to the facts of life, both at home and abroad, which were made under the imaginative and determined leadership of Franklin Roosevelt and Harry Truman. Our Republican friends evidently thought the definition of minority was the converse of maturity; that responsible conduct was not required until they attained majority status. Growing up is always a painful process. The necessity for doing so swiftly makes it worse.

There is, then, a unique opportunity for our party to achieve a new distinction. If we make the most of it, we not only best assure our own eventual triumph, but we may create a pattern of political conduct for others to see and follow, to the lasting benefit of the nation. For the party out of power, principle—and not patronage—must inevitably be the only solvent. Let us not fail to make a virtue of our necessity.

Yes, we Democrats have a special duty—we who chafed under the yoke of responsibility during the postwar years while Europe was saved and communism stopped—we who suffered all the while the taunts of irresponsible opposition. We must continue, I say, to tell the people the truth; that there are no magic, cheap, short solutions to global conflicts long in the making.

We must not yield to the temptation to goad the Republicans to produce quick miracles and dazzling successes. Let us never sow division when it is so important to harvest unity.

The tensions and difficulties may get worse before they get better in Europe, in the Middle East, in Asia—all around this world, divided and in revolution. Millions of people are as sorely puzzled as many of us here at home. The nature of the struggle is by no means clear to them and, unlike this heaven-favored land, there is lacking to many the same incentives to make the struggle. We must labor to increase these incentives, to prove to misery-laden millions that democracy can provide the right to think, to believe and to eat as well as vote.

That others have reservations about our unerring wisdom, that some cannot or will not fall in step at our pace must not exasperate and defeat us. And, in the dark majesty of the issue of life or death, none of us will advance our overriding interest in peace by outbursts of temper against each other or by ill-considered muscle-flexing against the common foe. We shall have to take care not to amuse our foes and frighten our friends.

Patience—firm, intelligent, understanding—seems to be in short supply. Yet it is the indispensable quality of leadership of the diverse elements of the free world and of the uncommitted millions groping their way into the sunlight of a better world. It is also the essential quality of a political party which, after the exhilaration of executive responsibility, finds itself in the less dramatic role of proving again its qualifications for public confidence.

What we, as a party, must cultivate is what the nation must have. In defeat, we can make ourselves servants of the national purpose for peace. There is no greater or better political destiny.

TRAVELER'S REPORT *From a radio broadcast made in Chicago, September 15, 1953.*

For six months, I have traveled across this vast and troubled world, for tens of thousands of miles—which were just as exhausting as the campaign, but I didn't encounter as much opposition! My mind is filled with recollections of people I talked with, from Syngman Rhee and the Emperor of Japan, to Pope Pius and Queen Elizabeth; of the sights I've seen, moving and beautiful, sordid and sickening; of the rugged front in ravaged Korea where, pray God, the strife has stopped for keeps; of the ugly war in the wet, green rice paddies of Indo-China where communism, masquerading as nationalism, imperils the whole of southeast Asia; and of millions of refugees huddled in squalid camps and hovels, stretching from Korea across Asia to western Europe—remnants of many more victims of the wars, revolutions, intolerance and savagery that have cursed our time on earth.

A trip like mine is a sobering experience. It is more than a privilege, it is a

responsibility to be an American in this world. It isn't one world; it's more like three worlds—the allied world, the Communist world, and the uncommitted world. Almost a billion people live along the route I took in 1953. Most of them live in Asia and most of the so-called uncommitted peoples live in Asia. They don't belong to the white minority of the human race, and tragically many of them are poor, undernourished and illiterate.

Asia is in revolution. Civilizations are very old, but political independence is very young. In the new states, the economies are shaky, public administration is weak; and they are hungry and poor, sensitive and proud. Nationalism is rampant. And the West, identified with the hated colonialism, is suspect. Utterly preoccupied with their own overwhelming problems, they see little of the world conflict and don't appreciate America's global responsibilities. They know from experience a lot about feudalism, landlords, money-lenders and oppressors, and the theories of Karl Marx sound pretty good to many of them, who know surprisingly little about the ugly realities of communism in practice. Nor is there the perception one would expect of the menace of international communism as a new imperialism.

There is little tradition of democracy in these new states, but independence, won at long last, is a passion, which partly accounts in some quarters for their opaque view of Communist China where, to many Asians, it appears that the foreigners have been thrown out and the ignominy of centuries erased by Asians. There is reverent admiration for the ideas of the American Revolution, the Bill of Rights, and the great utterances of human freedom. But they think they see contradictions in waves of conformity and fear here at home, and hypocrisy in our alliances with the colonial powers and professed devotion to freedom and self-determination.

The ideological conflict in the world doesn't mean much to the masses. Anti-Communist preaching wins few hearts. They want to know what we are for, not just what we are against. And in nations like India, Indonesia, and Burma, they don't accept the thesis that everyone has to choose sides, that they have to be for us or against us. Nor do I believe that we should press alliances on unwilling allies. After all, we had a long record of neutrality and non-involvement ourselves, and the important thing is that such nations keep their independence and don't join the hostile coalition.

But in spite of all their doubts and difficulties I was impressed by the devotion of the leaders of Asia to the democratic idea of government by consent rather than force, and by the decisive manner in which so many of the new countries of Asia have dealt with violent Communist insurrections and conspiracies. Their revolutions have not produced utopia and they are struggling with infinite difficulties to raise living standards and satisfy the rising tide of expectations. They want rice and respect, and they want to believe in wondrous America that sends friendly, earnest people to help them, and that believes in them and the aspirations of all God's children for peace, dignity and freedom.

We are on the eve of great decisions in Asia. Korea is the first step. Personally,

I have been skeptical of Red China's intentions, but when we search for settlements, we have to *search*, and when we negotiate, we have to have something to negotiate *with* as well as *for*. Many of our friends think China wants peace and trade above all, as they themselves do. With so much at stake in Asia—the unification of Korea, Formosa, peace and security in Indo-China—it would seem to me that we owe it to ourselves as well as to our friends at least to find out, if we can, what Communist China's ultimate intentions are.

If I may risk a prophecy, the hostile world is going to pay more and more attention to Asia, especially huge, uncommitted India. And I suspect that, as Europe's Eastern empires shrink, there will be left to us more of the burden of defense and of helping to guide the great forces which great changes have unleashed in Asia.

The Middle East is largely a power and defense vacuum, except for doughty little Israel and tough, strong Turkey. Peace is imperative in the Middle East—peace between the Arab states and Israel, which is engaged in an historic effort to provide refuge and new hope to oppressed people. □

The difficulties are many and the hazards great everywhere. But things are better. There is hope in the air, born of America's postwar policy of assistance and resistance, of growing strength and self-confidence, and of Stalin's death followed by shifting winds from Moscow, truce in Korea, rebellion in eastern Europe, troubles behind the iron curtain.

But the world is weary; there is universal anxiety and impatience to ease the tensions, to explore every possibility of settlements by conference and negotiation. The Soviet will exploit discord in our ranks at every opportunity in order to divide and enfeeble the grand alliance of the free. There is uncertainty abroad about America and our objective. Is our objective to discover, through negotiation, ways to relax tensions, or is it intensification of the cold war; is it coexistence or extermination of Communist power?

Some of the misunderstandings may seem incredible to us, but it is well to try to see ourselves as others see us. Many think we are intemperate, inflexible and frightened. And people who have lived in insecurity for centuries don't understand how there can be insecurity and fear in America which has never been bombed or lived in thralldom. Also, like ourselves, proud nations resent any real or suspected interference in their domestic affairs. Nor can they reconcile our exhortations about the peril with deep cuts in our defense budget. And everywhere people think they recognize the dominant mood of America in what is called "McCarthyism," now a world-wide word. Inquisitions, purges, book-burning, repression and fear have obscured the bright vision of the land of the free and the home of the brave.

Most of our friends want and need trade, not aid. There is an uneasy feeling that the United States is showing signs of economic nationalism, of a drift toward no trade and no aid. But our friends must trade to live, and not many are going to go hungry, I suspect, to prove to us just how anti-Communist they are.

Just as there are many misconceptions about us, we have many illusions about others, and one of them is that irritations, doubts and disagreements are symbols of ingratitude or anti-Americanism. Some hostile feeling is inevitable, particularly in occupied areas, but I found surprisingly little. Misgivings about our wisdom, unity and clear purpose, yes, but also widespread admiration and gratitude for our faith and fortitude, and prayerful hopes for the sobriety, good judgment and moral vitality of American leadership. At my journey's end, Winston Churchill said to me with emotion: "America has saved the world."

Our foreign assistance programs have succeeded, especially in Europe. They have cost us dearly, but I bless the day when President Truman went to the aid of Greece and Turkey and commenced the Marshall Plan. Stronger, more self-reliant, our friends are feeling more independent of Washington, and are talking back to us now, which seems to me a healthy sign.

I think we are winning the cold war, step by step. The spread of communism has been arrested. And while Moscow has military potency, the Communist idea has diminishing appeal, at least in Europe.

But though the imminent danger has receded, this is no time to wobble or lower our guards, not with the hydrogen bomb and no certain evidence that the seductive music from Moscow reflects any basic change in the Soviet design of world dominion. And it is no time for arrogance, petulance or inflexibility, either.

If I am not mistaken, holding our allies together is going to be an ever-harder job which will tax mightily our patience, resolve and statesmanship. For we can't "go it alone." Unilateralism is but the new face of isolationism, and it spells disaster.

Looking to the future, it seems to me clearer than ever that the economic, military and political integration of Europe is the best hope for balancing Soviet power and for enabling the states of Europe to exercise a powerful, positive and peaceful influence in the modern world. We have already invested years of effort and encouragement and billions of dollars toward this bold and imaginative end.

We must surmount a thicket of difficulty; we must bring the discussion back to the level where once again it challenges the imagination and the hopes of all Europe.

We must now think afresh; and, I believe, in terms of a European system of durable assurances of non-aggression—for Russia as well as for France, Germany and the rest of us. But whatever commitments we make to our European allies to buttress such assurances we must be prepared to make on a long-term basis. For there is anxiety lest the shaping of our policy may be slipping from the respected hands of President Eisenhower into the hands of men less concerned with strengthening our alliances abroad than with appeasing our isolationists at home.

And at this moment a new fact confers a grim and pressing urgency on the international situation—the hydrogen bomb. For some years efforts toward the limitation and control of armaments have been stalemated. Once more, I think, we should fix our sights high, as we did in 1947, and resume the initiative in re-exploring the possibility of disarmament. The alternative to safety through an effective plan for arms limitation is safety through more massive military spending and more frightening weapons development.

As it is, we seem now to be taking the initiative in unilateral disarmament. We've tried that before, and I am as opposed to unilateralism in our disarmament policy as I am in our foreign policy.

In the past new initiatives have had little impact on the Kremlin. I do not know that they would have any more today. But conditions have changed. The Soviet threat has aroused the massed military power of the free peoples. Russia learned in Korea that the West has the will to meet force with force. The death of Stalin and revolt in the satellites altered the situation inside the Soviet Union.

In these circumstances we should press forward—not under any foolish illusion that one grand conference would yield security, but rather with realistic recognition that the foundation of stability must be laid, stone by stone, with patient persistence. We owe it to ourselves and our anxious, weary friends to expose Communist intentions if we can, to confer when we can, to reduce tensions and restore hope where we can. The door to the conference room is the door to peace. Let it never be said that America was reluctant to enter.

McCARTHYISM *From a speech given at Miami Beach, March 6, 1954.*

This has been a fateful week in the history of American government. We are witnessing the bitter harvest from the seeds of slander, defamation and disunion planted in the soil of our democracy. □

It is wicked, it is subversive for public officials to try deliberately to replace reason with passion; to substitute hatred for honest difference; to fulfill campaign promises by practicing deception; and to hide discord among Republicans by sowing the dragon's teeth of discord among Americans. The loyalty, the patriotism of a whole political party, of one half of the nation, has been indicted. Twenty years of bipartisan effort, highly intelligent and highly successful, has been called "twenty years of treason" under the auspices of the Republican National Committee.

When one party says that the other is the party of traitors who have deliberately conspired to betray America, to fill our government services with Communists and spies, to send our young men to unnecessary death in Korea, they violate, not only the limits of partisanship; they also offend the credulity of our people, and they also stain the vision of America and of democracy for us and for the world that we seek to lead.

That such things are said under the official sponsorship of the Republican party in celebration of the birthday of Abraham Lincoln adds desecration to defamation. This is the first time that politicians, Republican politicians at that, have sought to split the Union—in Lincoln's honor.

This system of ours is wholly dependent upon a mutual confidence in the loyalty, the patriotism, the integrity of purpose of both parties. Extremism produces extremism, lies beget lies. The infection of bitterness and of hatred spreads all too quickly from one area to another of our life. And those who live by the sword of slander also may perish by it, for now it is also being used against

On February 29, 1956, President Eisenhower announced that despite his heart attack he would run for re-election that autumn. In a New York hotel room, Stevenson drafted a statement that read in part: "As the main issue will be the policies and record of the Eisenhower administration, it is fitting that President Eisenhower be the candidate. As the administration's chief architect and statesman, he will have to carry the burden of what will be a very rigorous campaign."

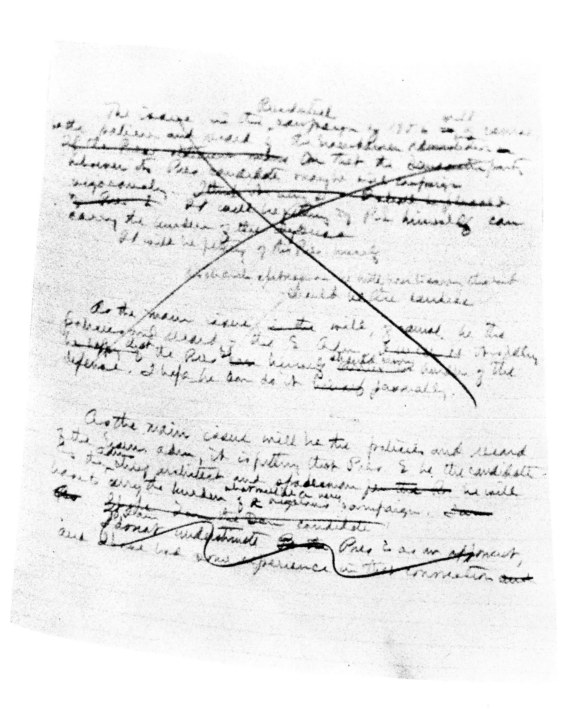

distinguished Republicans. We have just seen a sorry spectacle of this in the baseless charges hurled against our honored Chief Justice. And now, too, the highest officials of the Pentagon are charged with "coddling Communists" and "shielding treason."

General Zwicker, one of our great Army's finest officers, is denounced by Senator McCarthy as "stupid, arrogant, witless," as "unfit to be an officer" and a "disgrace to the uniform." For what? For obeying orders. This to a man who has been decorated thirteen times for gallantry and brilliance; a hero of the Battle of the Bulge. And this from a man whom the Republican National Committee sends around the country to sow slander and disunion—in memory of Abraham Lincoln.

When demagoguery and deceit become a national political movement, we Americans are in trouble; not just Democrats, but all of us.

Our State Department has been abused and demoralized. The American voice abroad has been enfeebled. Our educational system has been attacked; our press threatened; our servants of God impugned; a former President maligned; the executive departments invaded; our foreign policy confused; the President himself patronized; and now the integrity, loyalty and morale of the United States Army have been assailed.

For a moment, it looked as if this most recent audacity would at last meet effective resistance. But instead—well, what I might say as a Democratic partisan would have little value. But the pattern of this long series of aggressions against the Republic is clear and the consequences terrible.

The logic of all this is not only the intimidation and silencing of all independent institutions and opinions in our society, but the capture of one of our great instruments of political action—the Republican party. The end result, in short, is a malign and fatal totalitarianism.

And why, you ask, have the demagogues triumphed so often?

The answer is inescapable: because a group of political plungers has persuaded the President that McCarthyism is the best formula for political success.

Had the Eisenhower administration chosen to act in defense of itself and of the nation which it must govern, it would have had the grateful and dedicated support of all but a tiny and deluded minority of our people.

Yet, clear as the issue is, and unmistakable as the support, the administration appears to be helpless. Why? Because of the party's political ambitions. The administration is hopelessly, dismally, fatally torn and rent within itself.

It seems to me that this Stevens incident illustrates what preceding events have made memorably plain: a political party divided against itself, half McCarthy and half Eisenhower, cannot produce national unity; cannot govern with confidence and purpose. And it demonstrates that, so long as it attempts to share power with its enemies, it will inexorably lose power to them.

Perhaps you will say that I am making not a Democratic speech but a Republican speech; that I am counseling unity and courage in the Republican party and administration. You bet I am!

For, as Democrats, we don't believe in political extermination of Republicans, nor do we believe in political fratricide, in the extermination of one another. We believe in the Republic we exist to serve; and we believe in the two-party system that serves it—that can only serve it, at home and abroad—by the best and the noblest of democracy's processes.

RICH, RICH AMERICA *From a lecture at the University of Texas in September 1955.*

In terms of sheer material potency and well-being, we [in America] are without equal or precedent. Nor need there be any sense of guilt over this happy result; our living standards have not been gained by impoverishing others. Even back in the disagreeable old days before "Geneva," not even the Communists seriously claimed that! While material well-being may not be the first and is certainly not the only requisite for happiness, it surely helps. Man does not live by bread alone, but neither can he live without it. And nations who would help others must first have helped themselves.

Yet we know that nations, like men, have trouble wearing riches and power with grace. Indifference and arrogance have too often been the handmaidens of success. We are familiar with the temptation to attribute one's own accomplishments to virtue, and the misfortunes of others to a lack of diligence, brains or piety. Early in the present century, a prominent American industrialist stated that the interests of the workingmen would be protected, not, to use his term, by the "agitators," but "by the Christian gentlemen to whom God in his wisdom has entrusted the property interests of this country." He was not the first to confuse the prestige and power which go with the ownership of wealth with omniscience, virtue and even divinity. Rich nations have made the same mistake. History, in the end, has always proved them wrong. In the meantime they have not had or deserved the affection of the less fortunate.

We must not repeat this error. Humility and modesty, not pride or arrogance, must be the badges of our greatness. I do not think we are an arrogant or an immodest people, and certainly we have been a generous people. Let us so remain. □

Now how have we *used* our abundance? How have we worn our crown, how have we waved our scepter—imperiously and acquisitively, or humbly and generously? Here I think the record—the record of late years—is best of all.

We have—at least most of us—abandoned the illusions of isolationism, whose disastrous consequences following World War I we all know. (Although I can't overlook that many bitter and myopic authors of that policy long enjoyed public favor.) Latterly, many of us have been inclined to resent the burdens which world leadership imposes on us. We've been irritable and impatient and sometimes dangerously wrong as we strove to organize the free world against the Communist threat. But in general we have realized in effective action that our individual liberties, as well as our national security, require strong allies and our vigorous participation in all the affairs of the world in which we live. We have, in short, accepted the international obligations which our strength imposes upon us. We have decided wisely, I think, to use our economic power for peace, and peace, we have come to realize from the experience of two global wars, is indivisible in an interdependent world.

The cost to us has been enormous; and be it said to America's everlasting credit that we have asked nothing in return that we have not wished for all people —peace, security and well-being. While the record in Asia is less comforting, our foreign policy achievements, in short, are impressive and they disclose, on the whole, a generosity, a practicality, a concern for human values, and a respect for other peoples worthy of our great blessings and our colossal economic potency. And meanwhile, we Americans have also prospered, man for man, as never before.

Quite an achievement, indeed, in the past twenty years, and I say "on the whole," because we have not been without error. We have often obscured the purity of our purpose and created many false impressions of America—that it was selfish, acquisitive, irritable, erratic, belligerent and dangerous. And, of course, we have left no uncertainty about our preference for our way of doing things, whether applicable or not. □

In many places, friendly people in Asia, Africa, and Latin America are making vigorous efforts to help themselves—struggling to escape the vise of poverty, ignorance and disorder. In some countries, the progress is already apparent. In others, it is certain to come. But we can help to make progress both faster and far more certain. It is the margin that can make the difference between hope and hopelessness—for people with new visions of distant goals—poor people, overcrowded, underfed, illiterate and aware.

The future of mankind will be gravely affected by the outcome of this revolution. If the uncommitted third of the world ends in the Communist camp, freedom (and that means us) will have suffered a staggering blow. We can help these countries to help themselves and fulfill their aspirations in a framework of growing democracy and freedom. It would be the worst of all ironies if we, the richest land in the world, should stand on the sidelines and watch this fateful struggle go against us by default.

But we must not think of this aid only as saving these countries from communism. This is important, to be sure. It is more important for the countries concerned than for us. I doubt if any of them wish to fall within the Soviet orbit; none, I am sure, are staying out merely as a favor to the United States. We should justify our aid on the grounds of compassion and the sense of common humanity which make people at least a little different from animals. Idealism in modern times has not always been fashionable. Unless something can be justified by hardheaded self-interest, it is said to have no chance. But let us remember that kindness and idealism may be practical too, and, practical or not, they stand well in the eyes of God. □

Wealth has always had its responsibilities. This is so of individuals; life has rarely, and history never, been kind to those who refused to shoulder them. The case of nations is far more grave. The nation has in trust the well-being of its citizens. The great and powerful state has, in addition, custody of the welfare of other peoples. If wise and kind, it can be a good friend. If reckless or callous, it can damage or destroy.

History will measure the American performance, not by the treasure we pile up, but by the uses to which we put it. We will fulfill our destiny as a nation, not by materialism but by magnanimity. For the highest purpose of man and state, in the truly peaceful world we have never known, is to serve, not just our selfish aims, but the cause of mankind—for "above all nations is humanity."

So, at the end, when all our achievements have been cheered and all our debts have been acknowledged, our proper mood becomes a sober pride, a kind of solemn joy and self-respect in the recognition that "to whom much has been given, of him much shall be required."

We are left, I think, with a renewed understanding that the essence of our material power is a moral commitment whose maintenance against hostile outside pressures, and against our own inward corruption by the very power we wield, is our greatest mission as a people.

Stevenson with Senator Lyndon Johnson and newsmen at the Democratic convention's Texas suite in a Chicago hotel, August 1956.

V

THE LONG CAMPAIGN: 1956

CONVENTION PHOTOGRAPHS BY CORNELL CAPA
CAMPAIGN PHOTOGRAPHS BY JOHN FELL STEVENSON

By the summer of 1955, Stevenson had decided to seek the Democratic nomination the next year. The country's Democratic governors had given him warm encouragement when they gathered for a convention at Chicago, and his three sons agreed that he ought to run again, even though his chance of winning against Eisenhower was dim. He decided he would announce his candidacy in November. Then, in September, President Eisenhower had a serious heart attack. Democratic prospects changed drastically, for now it was likely that Nixon, not Eisenhower, would be the Republican nominee, and in those circumstances the Democratic nomination was a prize to be fought for. Some of Stevenson's support among Democrats cooled. In November he made his candidacy official ("which I suspect is hardly a surprise," he said). A month later Senator Estes Kefauver of Tennessee announced that he too would seek the nomination. Kefauver was a vigorous campaigner, and his coonskin hat and endless handshakes forced Stevenson into a long and demanding campaign simply to win the nomination, which in March ceased to look like such a prize when President Eisenhower announced he would run again. In August at the Democratic convention Stevenson won nomination on the first ballot, and Kefauver was picked as his running mate. The Democratic nominee for President had nine months of vigorous campaigning already behind him, and three months remained until the election.

In his acceptance speech Stevenson introduced his "New America" theme, a program of domestic reform which was the heart of his campaign. He hoped to stimulate serious debate, but the Republicans talked about "peace and prosperity" and avoided engaging with their opponent over the issues he raised. Probably the most debated so-called issue was Stevenson's proposal that the United States stop testing hydrogen bombs in the atmosphere. Scientific opinion supported him, but the lay public was persuaded by Republicans and a heavily Republican press that Stevenson's idea came dangerously close to unilateral disarmament. The Democrats certainly lost votes over the question. But within two years Eisenhower had admitted the dangers of fallout and asked for an end to atmospheric testing, not only of the large-yield hydrogen bombs, but of all nuclear devices.

Less than two weeks before the election—a time when normally candidates and issues dominate the headlines—the Middle East erupted into war. Israel invaded Egypt; England and France moved in to occupy the Suez Canal zone. The fact that the Suez crisis had been brought to the explosion point by American foreign policy blunders was not what concerned the headline-writers. The world was at the edge of war, the Western alliance had cracked apart, the Soviet Union had won a foothold in Egypt, and in the crisis the United States rallied behind its President. Eisenhower won a tidal-wave victory, carrying even seven states from the solid Democratic South.

THE DEMOCRATIC PARTY *From a telecast from Miami on May 26, 1956.*

Being a Democrat is for me a very great deal more than just being on a particular side of a lot of different issues.

I suppose there's no question about the fact that one reason I'm a Democrat —and mighty proud of it, incidentally—my father and grandfather before me were Democrats. I often think how much it is a measure of my political prejudice that inheritance always seems to me a good enough reason for being a Democrat but not a good enough reason for being a Republican.

But there is a lot more to it than this. I am a Democrat because I believe deeply in what the Democratic party stands for, and has stood for, for almost a century and a half. We sometimes forget that, while other political parties have come and gone, we who are Democrats today are members of the party of Thomas Jefferson and Andrew Jackson. We have become the party of centuries because we *do* have a central belief—and time has proved its soundness.

I can't put it in one word—although if I had to, that one word would be "people."

I find the heart of this belief in three statements you'll find in the history of the Democratic party—two of them, incidentally, by Democrats from the South.

It was Jefferson who said, 132 years ago, that "Men . . . are naturally divided into two parties; those who fear and distrust the people, and wish to draw all powers from them into the hands of the higher classes, and those who identify themselves with the people, have confidence in them as the most honest and safe . . . depository of the public interest."

Almost a century later, Woodrow Wilson said this: "When America loses its ardor for mankind, it is time to elect a Democratic President."

And, just last month in Washington, a great Democrat of today, Senator Herbert Lehman of New York, spoke of what he called "the passion for the full right of freedom."

What is at the heart of Democratic policy and principle and faith and belief? Well, we identify ourselves with people and have confidence in them; we have a fighting ardor for mankind; and we have a passion for the full right of freedom.

And these aren't just words. It seems to me that they offer clear and firm guidance to the most immediate and current problems we face today, yes, and to most of the issues in this election.

The present administration went into office proclaiming itself a businessman's government. The President's cabinet and most of the agencies of government have been filled with representatives of a single interest. I spoke in Fort Lauderdale last night of the policy of this administration not even to tell the rest of us, the people of this country, the truth about what is going on in our government and particularly in the handling of the issue of peace and war in the world. I say, with Thomas Jefferson, that this is wrong; that the government of this democracy cannot be one that distrusts the people and draws all powers from them into the hands of one class; that government in America *must* identify itself with *people*, have confidence in them, recognize *all* people—and no single group —as the only safe guardians of the public interest.

We are prosperous today as a nation. Yet in these last three and a half years, the administration in Washington has done nothing—or at least nothing substantial—about the human uses to which most of us want at least some part of this prosperity to be put.

Among the influential delegates who frequented the Stevenson suite in Chicago was Senator John F. Kennedy.

Among the influential delegates who frequented the Stevenson suite in Chicago was Senator John F. Kennedy.

Mrs. Edison Dick, Mrs. Eleanor Roosevelt and Stevenson discussing strategy for the convention in a car in front of the hotel that served as Democratic headquarters in Chicago.

We want better schools, more teachers, the hospitals we need, removal of the slums and the urban blight that breed juvenile delinquency. We want to keep the family farm as an essential part of our society. But these are basically human rather than business concerns—and this administration is utterly lacking, it seems to me, in what Woodrow Wilson called a "fighting ardor for mankind."

We want a program to make our older age a time of meaning, of dignity, of opportunity.

We Democrats do have a "fighting ardor for mankind"—and what this means to us is using the fruits of our prosperity in this land of plenty in this age of abundance, not to give tax cuts to large corporations, but to give us the things *we* want as *people*. Yes, and it means a program of dealing with the peoples of Asia and Africa and the Middle East in the realization that it is not war or military pacts that will defeat communism there, but a program rather that shows those people, too, that our ardor for mankind extends to *all* people.

Yes, and we Democrats have a *passion* for the *full* right of freedom. That's why we spoke out so strongly against the political attacks by Senator McCarthy and Vice-President Nixon on the Bill of Rights. That's why we have championed the idea of *free* trade unions and *free* collective bargaining. That's why we have felt so strongly and have been so critical about the failure of the present administration in Washington to recognize that in the Middle East this past year, not just one little nation, Israel, but the whole idea of freedom was being threatened by cynical aggravation of old tensions.

We don't just believe in freedom as an ideal; we've got a *passion*, as Senator Lehman puts it, for *full* freedom—that means what it's supposed to mean in people's everyday lives—here at home, yes, and in the whole world, for liberty knows no boundary lines, and tyranny won't stop at any border.

THE NEW AMERICA *Stevenson's theme for the campaign, summed up in a speech at Harrisburg, Pennsylvania, September 13, 1956.*

The Republicans pose the issues of this campaign in terms of slogans—"peace, prosperity, progress."

I pose these issues in terms of facts—the grim facts of America's unmet human needs, the facts of a revolutionary world in the hydrogen age.

Here are some facts:

In four years—four years of wealth and abundance—our government has let the shortage of schoolrooms and teachers get worse. It has done almost nothing to stop the slum cancer which today infects ten million American dwellings. And juvenile delinquency, which breeds in slums and poor schools, has increased at a frightening rate.

We have done nothing to help the lot of the poor and of our older people, most of whom must now subsist in a penury that gets worse as the cost of living climbs to the highest point in our history.

We have done precious little to aid the fight against cancer, arthritis, mental disease and other crippling and killing diseases, or to make up the shortage of doctors and nurses.

We have watched higher costs and lower prices close on the hapless, helpless farmer whose only offense is that he has done his job too well.

And the small businessman is now backed to the wall.

Instead of turning our natural resources—our rivers, lands and forest—to the public good, we have seen them raided for private profit.

And the facts of our progress toward peace are even more sobering. The Soviets have advanced, while we have fallen back, not only in the competition for strength of arms, but even in the education of engineers and scientists. Millions of people have moved more toward the false promises of communism than the true faith in freedom. And, today, there is doubt in the world about whether America *really* believes in the freedom which is our birthright and the peace which is our greatest hope.

Why has all this happened?

It has happened because, for four years now, we have had a government which neither fully understands nor wholly sympathizes with our human needs or the revolution that is sweeping the world.

The Republican administration took office on the pledge to make it a business-man's government. Well, that's one pledge they kept. President Eisenhower filled two out of every three top-ranking offices in his administration with men whose lives have been spent representing business, mostly big business.□

Now, I respect Mr. Eisenhower's good intentions. I have even been accused of undue moderation toward his administration. And certainly the Democrats in Congress have constantly rescued the Republican President from his own party.

Everyone shares in sympathy for the circumstances which have created a part-time presidency. But we cannot understand—and we will not accept—turning the government over to men who work full time for the wrong people or for a limited group of people.

And the plain truth is that this situation would get worse, not better; because what influence the President has with the Republican leaders in Congress has depended on his running again.

But from here on the future of Republican leaders will depend not on Mr. Eisenhower but on the Republican heir apparent, Mr. Nixon. And the Vice-President seems to sail downwind, no matter which way the wind blows.

These are stern facts. To ignore them is perilous. They are the reasons America's human needs today go unmet. Nor will they be met so long as the President is not master in his own house.

I firmly believe that America does not want to rest on dead center; that it wants—fervently—to move forward again to meet these needs. And I firmly believe that a leadership that will ask Americans to live up to the best that is in them will carry us across the threshold of the New America that now opens before us.

I think America wants to be called on to build the schoolrooms and train the

Mrs. Roosevelt supporting Stevenson in a talk to a state delegation at the convention. The giant photograph is of Truman, who opposed Stevenson's nomination.

teachers our children so desperately need.

I think America wants to be called to clear away the slums and bring basic decency to millions of American families.

I think America wants to attack relentlessly the vast realm of human pain, and lift from those hit by serious accident or illness at least the added burden of grinding debt.

I think America wants to give to the lives of people when they grow old the dignity and meaning they yearn for and deserve.

As I have in the past, I will lay before you, in as full detail as a campaign permits, proposals for meeting our needs. And we will talk soberly about their cost and ways and means of approaching them in a responsible manner.

Most of all we want peace. Whatever we can do here at home will be meaningless unless the world is such that what we do can endure.☐

It is not enough to pile pact on pact, weapons on weapons and to totter dangerously from crisis to crisis. There must be a call to war against the poverty, the hunger, the nothingness in people's lives that draws them to communism's false beacon.

We must guide the hopes of mankind away from the blind alleys of extreme nationalism or bogus Communist internationalism. We must turn them instead to an ideal of partnership between the nations in which disputes are settled by conciliation, not violence, and in which the weapons of death are limited and controlled. We Americans have never been and never will be a nation content just to count today's blessings.

We have confidence in ourselves, confidence that we can build what we have to build, grow as we have to grow, change as we must change, and play our full part in the making of a New America and a better tomorrow for ourselves and all mankind.

Our plan for twentieth-century man is not just for his survival but for his triumph.

If I were to attempt to put my political philosophy tonight into a single phrase, it would be this: Trust the people. Trust their good sense, their decency, their fortitude, their faith. Trust them with the facts. Trust them with the great decisions. And fix as our guiding star the passion to create a society where people can fulfill their own best selves—where no American is held down by race or color, by worldly condition or social status, from gaining what his character earns him as an American citizen, as a human being and as a child of God.

THE ISSUES OF THIS CAMPAIGN *From a speech made at Yale University, October 5, 1956.*

I am not opposed to a hard fight. Indeed, there are some who seem to think I have been fighting too hard in this campaign.

I was somewhat consoled the other day, however, when an old friend, comparing the 1956 campaign with 1952, said—a bit sourly, I thought—"I am glad at last to see the declarative sentence begin to triumph over the subjunctive."

Hard-hitting factual debate is the essence of democracy. Innuendo, smear and slander are not. They debauch the language of politics; they defile the dialogue which is the means by which free society governs itself. George Orwell once said that if you want to corrupt a people, first corrupt the words in which they express themselves. The English language can take a lot, especially in election year, but there are limits to the burden of deceit and infamy which it should be asked to bear.

This is a point in the campaign when it seems worth recalling the ground rules of political responsibility—and I mean in terms of self-reminder as much as criticism. I can only say that, in the heat of battle, even the obvious sometimes becomes blurred and worth reasserting.

Perhaps there is too much of the commonplace in the old injunction that victory is, after all, not an end in itself. Yet I often think that the single greatest difficulty about running for responsible public office is how you can win without, in the process, proving yourself unworthy of winning.

Don't misunderstand me; I mean to win in November.

But the perception that you can pay too great a price for victory—that the means you use may destroy the principles you think you cherish—is fundamental to democratic responsibility.

If the rule itself seems over-obvious—that there is something more to political accomplishment than electoral victory—then let me suggest two propositions that are both its corollary and its test.

First, I don't believe any victory is worth winning in a democracy unless it can be won by placing full trust in the members of the democracy.

I mean giving people the hard facts and the hard decisions—trusting their sobriety and their judgment—regarding them not as the customers of government, to be sold, but as the owners of government, to run their own affairs.

I mean resisting today's temptations to rely on soft soap, slogans, gimmicks, bandwagons and all the other infernal machines of modern high-pressure politics in this age of mass manipulation.

The promise of such manipulations is contempt—contempt for people's intelligence, common sense and dignity.

The second corollary is that the political party can never be considered an end in itself. It is only an agency for a larger purpose.

Again, let no one misunderstand me. I believe in party loyalty and party responsibility. I am a Democrat, a good party Democrat, a very proud Democrat. But that very pride depends upon my heartfelt conviction that this party is an instrument for carrying out certain principles for the establishment of certain values. What is of fundamental and lasting importance is the ideals a party incarnates, and the purpose of the party is to make government serve our lives as it should serve them.

It is easy and proper and very right to assert that the fortunes of our party are, in the long view, closely and integrally related to our national welfare. Our long history of public service—its many contributions to that welfare in time of crisis, domestic and foreign—can leave no doubt of this. What is more important is to be sure we keep it always in mind that the fortunes of our party, even in the short run, are of infinitely less importance than the national interest as it is conceived by all our citizens, in and out of direct party affiliation or allegiance.

Surely it is appropriate for us to consider the issues that face us in those terms.

The most important fact about any year, including the quadrennial one of national election, is its own identity, its standing apart in its own niche in time, its own remoteness from the years that have gone before, its uniqueness as the only gateway through which we may enter into the years ahead.□

Is it not the very essence of greatness, in a person as in an institution, to face squarely the often uncomfortable fact that the world moves on with the inexorable succession of the years? New problems arise, new challenges are presented and, most important of all, new opportunities are provided which, if not seized upon with courage and energy and imagination, are shouldered aside by the relentless cycle of time.

I do not believe that we Democrats have the answers for 1956 simply because we had them for 1932. No more do I believe that the Republicans have them for this present moment in time simply because the country turned to them in 1952. And the greatest mistake we, as a people, could make would be to confuse 1956 with 1952 simply because the same two individuals are carrying the party standards.

As one of those individuals, I am peculiarly exposed to the temptation of thinking that the issues are the same because the faces are the same. But I try to resist it because I know that to yield is to defy the overriding law of life, which is change. And the way I resist is by continually asking myself: What is this election really all about this year? What are the watchwords of the past which have no relevance for the present? What should we be thinking, planning, initiating, doing—now?

I think the central issue in 1956, particularly for the uncommitted voter, is that complacency contains the seeds of decay, not of growth. It is at war with our national genius. It falsifies the tradition which has taken shape in sharp and glowing outline throughout our 180 years as an independent people. In the few periods when its siren song has been heard most loudly in the land, it has been a prelude to a harsher melody in which the saddest note is one of mourning for what might have been.

We have heard a very great deal and we are going to hear much in the weeks ahead about prosperity and peace. But surely the uneven measure of prosperity we now enjoy and the restless and uneasy peace in which we now find ourselves were not achieved by standing still and admiring them. We have become the world's envy because we never stopped raising our sights, because we constantly set new goals for ourselves even as we gained the old, because pretty good was never good enough.

In our hearts we know we must be up and doing, probing ceaselessly for new breakthroughs in our endless striving for solutions for today's problems and for the new ones that tomorrow will find on our doorstep, searching always for better answers than the ones we have been able to come up with thus far. We

The candidate accepts the Democratic nomination, August 16, 1956.

The Democrats unite: Kefauver, Harriman, Stevenson and Truman on the platform at the convention.

84

know that the gospel of discontent is the prophet of progress.

It is our mood that is the issue in this election. From whence is to come the energy to quicken it, the vision to excite it, the courage and will to lead it—to goad it, if need be—forward toward the greater fulfillment it has always demanded?

The essence of our faith is the determination to measure today's problems, not against yesterday's fears, but against tomorrow's hopes.

To you, the young among us, I say that your generation confronts a baffling and difficult world. Your problems are not those of my generation. Your task is infinitely more difficult. It is not just to find a job for yourself—it is to save a world, a world in revolution. Your task is not to recover a faith, but to give that faith reality.

There have been revolutionary intervals before. They are times of danger and of opportunity—grave danger and exhilarating opportunity.

You know that America can conquer crippling disease, can discover creative uses for the new leisure which will come in the wake of abundance, can transform our surpluses into a blessing to mankind rather than a burden to the farmers, can strike a mighty blow at the ancient curse of poverty, and can achieve for all Americans that individual freedom, that equality of opportunity and that human dignity which belong to them as American citizens and as children of God.

You know, too, that America can restore its position in the world, that it can become once again a trusted and inspiring leader, dedicated not to keeping things as they are, but to making the promise of our own revolution a light for all mankind. You know that we can lead the peoples of the earth away from the false beacons of communism and slavery to a new age of human abundance and human fulfillment.

Our national purpose is not just to have an election and get it out of the way. Our purpose is not to watch a horse race in which all we care about is victory and at almost any price. Our purpose is to show how a great nation rises to the responsibility of self-government—and how it emerges from the experience purified in purpose, strengthened in resolution and united in faith.

AMERICA'S FOREIGN POLICY *From a speech in Washington, D.C., April 21, 1956, before Stevenson had won the nomination again.*

Now, where are we today? At this period of an extraordinary age which has witnessed the coincidence of three revolutions:

1. The technological revolution that has split the atom, devastated distance and made us all next-door neighbors.

2. The political revolutions that have liberated and subjugated more peoples more rapidly than ever before in history.

3. The ideological revolution, communism, that has endangered the supremacy of Western ideas for the first time since Islam retreated from Europe.

It is against this background of violent, sudden change in all directions that the drama—or melodrama—of foreign policy must be played. This is a time of change in world affairs. The peoples sense it, even if the statesmen don't, for the peoples are, in a deep sense, forcing change. No one knows just where these changes will lead.

The administration has been slow to respond to this new mood. The Russians, on the other hand, have exploited it adroitly. Their objectives, we are told almost every day, have not changed. Of course they haven't. No one said they had. The Soviet rulers frankly state that their goal is a Communist world. But they have changed their approach; and we have not changed ours.□

I do not propose to chronicle here the whole long list of tension points in the world today. We know their names: Israel, Algeria, Formosa, Indochina and Indonesia, Kashmir, Cyprus and now the whole NATO area.

What is more basic and ominous and infinitely harder for us to accept is that, in these last three years, the United States has come dangerously close to losing, if indeed it has not lost, its leadership in the world—economically, militarily and, worst of all, morally. On all three of these fronts, we have manifestly lost the initiative—and that is the prelude to the loss of leadership itself.

It is tragic irony that the people of America, who believe more firmly and fervently in peace and human freedom than anyone else, are not recognized as their sympathetic friends by the millions of mankind who are struggling out of the poverty and squalor and colonial bondage of ages. Instead, it is Communist imperialism which has enslaved scores of millions in a decade, which is usurping the role.

And, only a few years back, we seemed to those people the hope of the earth! America had gained freedom itself through revolution against European colonialism. Our great documents, from the Declaration of Independence to the Atlantic Charter, had spoken the aspirations of independence and growth. Our own colonial policies had been generous and forbearing. Our great leaders had affirmed the ideals of freedom with an eloquence that had won the allegiance of men and women everywhere. It was to us that new nations instinctively looked for sympathy, for support and for guidance.

Yet today, in the great arc from North Africa through Southeast Asia, the Russian challenge is developing rapidly and with great flexibility and force. Everywhere people, seeking a short cut to raise their own standards of life, are told that the Soviet Union alone has mastered the secret of converting a peasant economy into a modern industrial state in a single generation.

In the meantime we, whose position is fundamentally decent and honorable and generous, have so mismanaged ourselves of late that we must now try to prove that we love peace as much as the Russians, and are as concerned with the problems of economic development and national independence as they are. It is fantastic but true.□

I trust I've made it clear that armed might should not stand as the symbol of our foreign policy. But military power is diplomacy's indispensable partner during this period when the ramparts of peace are still to be built and genuine arms control is still in the future.

To summarize: Three years ago, this nation was looked to by all the free world as equipped by faith, history, accomplishment and authority to lead the peoples of the world to the promised land of security and peace. That is no longer the case. And we must squarely face the fact that there is no time to lose in re-examining and in redefining our policy to meet the challenge of today.

I know well the willfulness of the forces which affect the conduct of a nation's foreign policy. I make no pretense that there are one or two or three sure steps which would solve our problems. Wars may be won by secret weapons, but there are no secret weapons which will guarantee peace.

But I recognize the obligation to measure criticism by affirmative suggestion. So let me make some suggestions which are inherent, I think, in what I have said.

First of all, a decent respect for the opinions of others is still a basic require-ment of a good foreign policy. Foreign policy is not only *what* we do, it is *how* we do it. The wisest policy will be poisonously self-defeating if mishandled. Smugness, arrogance, talking big are poison. Impulsive, abrupt actions create the impression that we are impulsive and abrupt. The restoration of composure, confidence and an impression of knowing-what-we-are-about is thus of first im-portance.

We want to be recognized not as bold, but as prudent, and that rules out boasting about brinks and the like. We want to be recognized as sensitive to the implications of modern warfare, and that rules out talk of massive retaliation. We want to be recognized as responsible, and that rules out trying to reconcile the irreconcilable wings of the Republican party. We want to be regarded as reasonable, and that rules out nonsense about the imminent collapse of the Soviet system. And we must reveal that craving for peace which is the true heart of America.

Second, I believe we should give prompt and earnest consideration to stopping further tests of the hydrogen bomb, as Commissioner Murray of the Atomic Energy Commission recently proposed. As a layman, I hope I can question the sense in multiplying and enlarging weapons of a destructive power already almost incomprehensible. I would call upon other nations, the Soviet Union, to follow our lead, and if they don't and persist in further tests, we will know about it and we can reconsider our policy.

I deeply believe that if we are to make progress toward the effective reduction and control of armaments, it will probably come a step at a time. And this is a step which, it seems to me, we might now take, a step which would reflect our determination never to plunge the world into nuclear holocaust, a step which would reaffirm our purpose to act with humility and a decent concern for world opinion.□

Third, we should seriously consider basic revision of our method of giving aid; specifically, we should, I think, make greater use of the United Nations as the economic aid agency. We should try to remove economic development from the arena of the cold war. We believe, to be sure, that anything which strengthens economic growth, national independence, human welfare and democratic processes will improve a nation's resistance to the virus of communism. But our first purpose is human betterment, and anything else is a by-product.

Also, if we propose to make economic aid most effective, we will have to stop demanding that recipient nations pass loyalty tests, and stop using our money to bribe feeble governments to set up rubber-check military pacts which will bounce as soon as we try to cash them. Rather, we must convince the peoples of the underdeveloped world that we want no dominion over them in any form, and that we look forward to the end of colonialism in the world.

I don't believe we have explored all possible uses of our agricultural surpluses as raw materials of diplomacy. Surely there are ways of using our abundance, not as an embarrassment, but creatively as part of a comprehensive plan of foreign assistance.

There is, too, the vast potential in peaceful use of atomic energy. It will be our ultimate ironical failure if the Soviet Union, rather than the United States, should provide the underdeveloped needful nations with atomic power. Our mastery of the atom, our willingness to make it mankind's public utility, should be one of our greatest contributions to human betterment.

I emphasize again, however, that all the bushels of wheat and the nuclear reactors and dollars in creation will do us little good if they seem only to be the bait with which a rich but uncertain nation seeks to buy protection for itself. If our attitude is wrong, no amount of money can do the job; and if our attitude is right, less money will go further.

These poor nations have discovered that poverty, oppression and disease are not the immutable destiny of man. They mean to improve their lot and quickly —by the methods of consent, our Western way, if possible. But if they can't, they will turn away from us—to forced labor and forced savings, the totalitarian way—because they mean to industrialize one way or another.□

Finally, it seems to me that any aid program we devise will be effective, only as it expresses a healthy relationship between free and self-respecting peoples. We must show that we care about others in the world, not as bodies we would hurl into the military breach, but as men and women and children who we hope will live lives of dignity and fulfillment.

So long as we overmilitarize our international thought and statement, so long as we picture the differences between Russia and the West as part of a great military contest, hot or cold—for so long will our efforts prove futile and our motives suspect. For there is little about that struggle which penetrates the minds and hearts of the people of Asia or Africa.

Let us, rather, rally the nations for a world-wide war against want. And let us then—for men do not live by bread alone—identify what we do in the world with the one export which we can offer as no one else can. I mean liberty, human freedom, independence, the American idea—call it what you please—which is more precious and more potent than guns or butter.

For from the word "go"—which is to say, from our very first national state-ment in 1776—America spoke for freedom in terms so inspiring, so sublime and

Stevenson and Truman shake hands just after Stevenson's nomination. Behind them is Paul Butler, the Democratic national chairman.

Stevenson and Truman shake hands just after Stevenson's nomination. Behind them is Paul Butler, the Democratic national chairman.

Mrs. Roosevelt and a group of girls for Stevenson at the convention in Chicago.

The Democratic nominees: Stevenson and Estes Kefauver.

so inexorably appealing to men's consciences that the Old World was shaken to its foundations. Tyrannies dissolved; hope sprang up like a fresh breeze; movements of liberation mushroomed. This was the greatest foreign aid program in history, and no one has ever improved on it or ever will.

WAR IS OBSOLETE *One of the noisiest issues of the campaign was Stevenson's proposal to halt the testing of hydrogen bombs. This was his feeling about nuclear weapons voiced in a speech on May 24, 1955, more than a year before the campaign officially began.*

With the unlocking of the atom, mankind crossed one of the great watersheds of history. We have entered uncharted lands. The maps of strategy and diplomacy by which we guided ourselves until yesterday no longer reveal the way. Fusion and fission revolutionized the entire foundation of human affairs. It has placed mankind, in the words of Sir Winston Churchill, "in a situation both measureless and laden with doom."

The words we use when we talk of this terrible force are so absolute as to be almost meaningless. We say that civilization cannot survive an atomic war, that there can be no victory and no victors, that nuclear weapons can annihilate all life on this planet. All these statements are true. But it is nearly impossible for us to understand them.

This scientific revolution in man's capacity for self-destruction calls for an equivalent revolution in man's capacity for self-preservation and the conduct of our foreign affairs. It will not do to rely only on the orthodox, time-tried methods of foreign policy which the great states have used in the past; for war was one of these methods; and today either war must become obsolete, or mankind will.

In the long run, nothing will meet the needs of the people of our nation or of the world short of abolishing the very institution of war as an arbiter of disputes or a tool of annihilation.

We must, of course, continue to preserve and to build our alliances, to help free nations gain strength to preserve their freedom, to develop our own armed strength—indeed, until the aggressors come to tolerable terms, we must even continue building our own nuclear power.

But this is not enough. To stop here is to dwell still in the house of the past, with a bomb ticking in the basement. We can no longer rest contentedly on the framework of the old diplomacy and the old strategy of preponderant or balanced power. We must move beyond to that brighter day envisioned just ten years ago when the Nazi nightmare died and the United Nations came to birth in San Francisco amid great rejoicing. We must resume the attack on the institution of war itself.

Let no one deceive himself about the enormity of this task. The roots of war lie deep, not only in rivalries among peoples and conflicts among nations and ideas, but in the dark tormented depths of the human heart. To abolish human rivalry and conflict would be a utopian dream. But to try and make sure that human rivalry and conflict will not abolish us is not just a possibility; it is an imperative necessity.

The differences between ourselves and the Communists are great and terrifying. They will not be easily resolved. I doubt if they will be resolved in our lifetime. Our effort must be to make sure that their resolution will take place not in the old arena, where war was one of the weapons, but in a new arena, under new rules, in a new spirit and the effort must be remorseless.□

What are the chances that we may get somewhere at last in our efforts to prevent a hydrogen war? I don't know. While there are signs that patience and strength are paying off, I have no illusions that our search for peace will succeed easily. Yet, in all conscience, our great nation has no choice other than to use its day of leadership to work remorselessly for peace—to do its best to make sure that the epoch of American power produces not the final earthly holocaust, but a world of justice, security and freedom.

Faith, knowledge and peace—these will be the cornerstones of such a world. And, of these, none will avail if peace is lacking, if an atom split in anger turns out to be mankind's last reality.

TESTING BOMBS *Here are Stevenson's feelings on this issue in the thick of campaigning, October 15, 1956.*

We are caught up today, along with the rest of the world, in an arms race which threatens mankind with stark, merciless, bleak catastrophe.

It is no accident that the instinct of survival which is common to all men and all nations is slowly but surely compelling the most practical and hardheaded statesmen to give increasing heed to the prevention and abolition of war. In this nuclear age, peace is no longer merely a visionary ideal; it has become an urgent and practical necessity.

Yet we dare not tear down and abandon armed deterrents to war before we devise and secure other and more effective guaranties of peace. Great and law-abiding nations cannot leave their security at the mercy of others. We have learned that unilateral disarmament invites rather than deters aggression.

So, until there is world-wide agreement on an effective system of arms reductions with adequate safeguards, we must maintain our national defense and the defenses of the free world.

I am not only opposed to unilateral disarmament, but I have felt that we should not put too many of our eggs in the atomic and hydrogen basket. I have felt that we should try to maintain sufficient balance, flexibility and mobility in our armed strength so that we will not be forced to choose between appeasement and massive retaliation, between too little and too much, between submission and holocaust.

Effective disarmament means universal disarmament—an open world, with no secret armies, no secret weapons, and, in effect, no military secrets. Responsible statesmen do not risk the security of their countries for hopes which may prove illusory or promises that are worthless.

But nations have become so accustomed to living in the dark that it is not easy for them to learn to live in the light. And all our efforts to work out any safe, reliable, effective system of inspection to prevent evasion of arms agreements have been blocked by the Soviet rulers. They won't agree to let us inspect them; we cannot agree to disarm unless we can inspect them. And the matter has been deadlocked there for eleven years.

Yet, if we are going to make any progress, we must find means of breaking out of this deadly deadlock. We must come forward with proposals which will bear witness to our desire to move toward and not away from disarmament.

It was with this hard, urgent need in mind that I proposed last spring that all countries concerned halt further tests of large-size nuclear weapons—what we usually call the H-bombs. And I proposed that the United States take the lead in establishing this world policy.

I deliberately chose to make this proposal as far removed as possible from the political arena. It was made four months before the party conventions. It was made to the American Society of Newspaper Editors. It was made without criticism of the present administration's policy for H-bomb development.

Others—and not I—have chosen to make this proposal for peace a political issue. But I think this is good. After all, the issue is mankind's survival, and man should debate it, fully, openly and in democracy's established processes.

Because there has been only negative criticism of this proposal from the Republican candidates in this campaign, I want to return to it tonight.

These are the reasons why I think the time is ripe and there is an insistent necessity for the world to stop at least the testing of these terrifying weapons:

First, the H-bomb is already so powerful that a single bomb could destroy the largest city in the world. If every man, woman and child on earth were each carrying a 16-pound bundle of dynamite—enough to blow him to smithereens and then some—the destructive force in their arms would be equal to the force of one 20-megaton hydrogen bomb, which has already been exploded.

Second, the testing of an H-bomb anywhere can be quickly detected. You can't hide the explosion any more than you can hide an earthquake.

As the President has stated: "Tests of large weapons, by any nation, may be detected when they occur." In short, H-bomb testing requires no inspection. We will know it when it happens anywhere and, by studying the dust from that explosion, we can even determine what progress the other country has made.

This means that if any country broke its pledge, we would know it and could promptly resume our own testing.

Third, these tests themselves may cause the human race unmeasured damage.

With every explosion of a superbomb, huge quantities of radioactive material are pumped into the air currents of the world at all altitudes—later to fall to earth as dust or in rain. This radioactive fallout carries something called strontium 90, which is the most dreadful poison in the world. Only a tablespoon, shared equally by all members of the human race, would produce a dangerous level of radio-

The campaign begins.

activity in the bones of every individual. In sufficient concentration, it can cause bone cancer and dangerously affect the reproductive processes.

Prior to the atomic age, radioactive strontium was practically nonexistent in the world. Careful studies show that today all of us—all over the world—have some of it in our bones. It enters our bodies through the foodstuffs grown in soil on which the bomb dust has fallen.

I do not wish to be an alarmist and I am not asserting that the present levels of radioactivity are dangerous. Scientists do not know exactly how dangerous the threat is. But they know the threat will increase if we go on testing. And we should remember that less than half of the strontium created by past tests by Russia and the United States has as yet fallen to earth from the stratosphere.

So it seems clear to me that, if it is humanly possible, we should stop sending this dangerous material into the air just as soon as we can!

Fourth, the dangers of testing by three powers are ominous enough, but there is another reason why it is important to act now. Last May, Mr. Stassen, the President's disarmament assistant, said that within a year the "secret" of making the hydrogen bomb would spread around the world. Think what would happen if a maniac, another Hitler, had the hydrogen bomb. And imagine what the consequences would be of a dozen nations conducting hydrogen bomb tests and wantonly thrusting radioactive matter into the atmosphere.

These are the reasons why it seems to me imperative that a world policy of stopping these tests be established at the very first possible moment.

I proposed last April that the United States take the initiative toward this end by announcing our willingness to stop these tests, "calling upon other nations to follow our lead," and making it clear that, unless they *did*, we would have to resume our experiments too. That was my proposal. It was simple. It was safe. It was workable.

And, since that time, both Russia and Great Britain have declared their willingness to join us in trying to establish the kind of policy I have suggested.

What are we waiting for? □

I say that America should take the initiative; that it will reassure millions all around the globe who are troubled by our rigidity, our reliance on nuclear weapons and our concepts of massive relatiation, if mighty magnanimous America spoke up for the rescue of man from the elemental fire which we have kindled.

As we all know, in the world in which we live, only the strong can be free. Until we succeed in abolishing the institution of war itself, we must have, together with our allies, the strength to deter aggression and to defeat it if it comes. That is the first condition of peace in an armed world.

One last word.

The search for peace will not end, it will begin, with the halting of these tests.

What we will accomplish is a new beginning, and the world needs nothing so much as a new beginning.

Stevenson and Willard Wirtz working on a speech in mid-flight.

A WORLD WITHOUT WAR *Seven years later, Stevenson's feelings about nuclear weapons had not changed. This is from a statement to the Political Committee of the United Nations, November 15, 1961.*

War is one of the oldest institutions. It is deeply imbedded in the traditions, the folkways, the literature, even the values of almost all countries. It has engaged countless talented men and produced countless national heroes. At the same time, civilized men and women for centuries past have abhorred the immorality of organized killing of men by men.

Yet, let us confess at once, to our common shame, that this deep sense of revulsion has not averted wars, nor shortened one by a day.

While I do not say that all wars have been started for unworthy purposes, let us also confess, morality to the side, that almost all past wars have served to promote what was conceived to be the national or princely or religious interests of those who fought them—or at least those who won them.

For in past wars, there have been winners as well as losers, the victors and the vanquished, the decorated and the dead. In the end, valuable real estate and other riches have changed hands. Thrones have been won, regimes transferred, rule extended, religions and ideologies imposed, empires gained and lost, aggressions halted or advanced.

Thus, wars in the past have sometimes been a means of settling international disputes, of changing political control, of inducing social transformation and even of stimulating science and technology.

And I suppose that, on moral grounds, it is only a difference of degree whether millions are killed or only thousands, whether the victims include children in the debris of a big city building or only young men lying on a battlefield in the countryside.

Nor has war been a very efficient way of settling disputes. Yesterday's enemies are today's friends. First, the victor pays for destruction of his enemy, then for reconstruction of his friend.

But war in the future would differ fundamentally from war in the past, not in degree but in kind. It is this which seems so difficult to grasp. Thermonuclear war cannot serve anyone's national interest—no matter how moral or immoral that interest may be, no matter how just or unjust, no matter how noble or ignoble, regardless of the nation's ideology, faith or social system.

It is no satisfaction to suggest that the issue of morality in war thus has become academic. Yet this is the fact and perhaps it will serve to clarify the dialogue of war and peace. For we can now free our collective conscience of nice ethical distinctions, and face the stark amoral fact that war has ceased to be practical, that no nation can contemplate resort to modern war except in defense against intolerable exaction or aggression. Therefore, we must abolish war to save our collective skins. For as long as this nuclear death dance continues, millions— tens of millions—perhaps hundreds of millions—are living on borrowed time.

I suggested that war is such an ancient institution, so deeply entrenched in tradition, that it requires a strenuous intellectual effort to imagine a world free

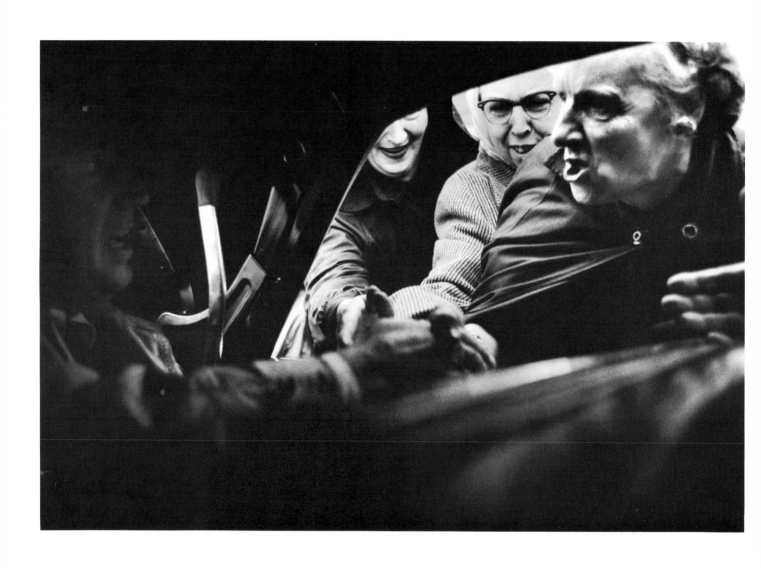

from war. So it does. But I submit that the alternative effort is to imagine a world at the end of another war; when great areas and great places have been turned into radioactive wasteland; when millions upon millions of people are already dead, while debris from those great mushroom clouds drifts ghoulishly over the living; when great parts of our institutions, ideologies, faiths and beliefs, even our art and literature, lie smashed in the smoke and rubble of material destruction.

I submit that, however difficult the vision of a world *without war* may be, it is not only a happier but an easier vision to imagine than one of a world *after war*. In any event, we must choose between them.☐

In a world without arms, military power would be taken out of the hands of nations; but other forms of power would remain, and mostly in the hands of the same states which are the most powerful military states today.

Conflicting ideologies would still be with us.

Political struggles would still take place.

Social systems would still be subject to disruptive pressures from within and without.

Economic strength would still be a factor in, and an instrument of, national foreign policies.

And the world would still be the scene of peaceful transformations, for it cannot and should not remain static.

Let us be clear about all this:

Disarmament alone will not purify the human race of the last vestiges of greed, ambition and brutality, of false pride and the love of power. Nor will it cleanse every last national leader of the least impulse to international lawlessness. No sane and honest man can pretend to foresee such a paradise on earth—even an earth without arms. But it would be a safer earth, where the contest and conflict could be waged in peace.

Obviously, then, disarmament will not usher in utopia. But it will prevent the wanton wastage of life and the wholesale destruction of material resources. And it will free the energies of man to engage in beneficent pursuits. How much could be done to improve the conditions of man—his education, his health, his nutrition and his housing—even if a small portion of the funds and the ingenuity of man now devoted to improving the art of killing were transferred to improving the art of living!

Who would keep the peace in a disarmed world? How would our disputes get settled when arms have been taken away?

If we can answer these questions, we are much nearer to a solution of the problem of disarmament. For these are questions that open up the unexplored ground between first steps toward disarmament and the vision at the end of the road. And the vision of a world free from war will remain a utopian illusion until means for keeping the peace lend it reality.

It therefore seems clear to me that the only way to general and complete disarmament lies along two parallel paths which must be traveled together. One leads to the absence of arms, the other to the presence of adequate machinery for

Stevenson and William McC. Blair, Jr., watching the election returns on television. The screen shows Eisenhower having won 42 states and 478 electoral votes to Stevenson's 6 states and 61 electoral votes. The final figures next day were actually 41 and 457 for Eisenhower to 7 and 74 for Stevenson.

keeping the peace. As we destroy an obsolete institution for the settlement of disputes, we must create new institutions for the settlement of disputes—and simultaneously.

Let me repeat for emphasis. We do not hold the vision of a world without conflict. We do hold the vision of a world without war, and this inevitably requires an alternative system for coping with conflict. We cannot have one without the other. But if we travel the two roads together—if we build as we destroy—we can solve the vast technical problems here involved. □

A world disarmed would not be utopia, but one suddenly blessed by freedom from war. It would not usher in world government, but the world community would have the capacity to keep the peace. It would not end national sovereignty, but the sovereign right to commit national suicide would be yielded up forever.

A disarmed world would still be a world of great diversity, in which no one nation could seriously pretend to have the wit and wisdom to manage mankind. It would be a world in which ideas, for the first time, could compete on their own merits without the possibility of their imposition by force of arms. It would be a world in which men could turn their talents to an agenda of progress and justice for all mankind in the second half of the twentieth century. In short, it would not be a perfect world, but a world both safer and more exhilarating for us all to live in.

There is nothing inherently impossible in creating the conditions for a world without war. Our basic problems are not technical, mechanistic or administrative. The basic question is whether every nation will agree to abandon the means to coerce others by force.

If they will not, the arms race will go on. For those who love freedom and have the power to defend it will not be coerced. And uncertain as it is, free people prefer to live on borrowed time than to yield to terror.

Conceivably, the world could survive on this perpetual brink of universal disaster. Conceivably, fortune would spare us from the fatal act of a lunatic, the miscalculation of an uninformed leader, the false step of a nervous young sentry.

But on behalf of my government and my people I propose that this Assembly set the world on the road toward freedom from war.

And I propose that this committee take the first steps by approving a negotiating forum, endorsing the statement of agreed principles already worked out by the United States and the Soviet Union, and recommending that the new forum get on at once with the first business of this dangerous world—general and complete disarmament.

I ask the Soviet delegate whether his country cannot so conduct negotiations now that we and our respective allies may be able to turn to the rest of the members here, and to the hundreds of millions for whom they speak, and say: "We have not failed you."

Two o'clock in the morning, after his defeat.

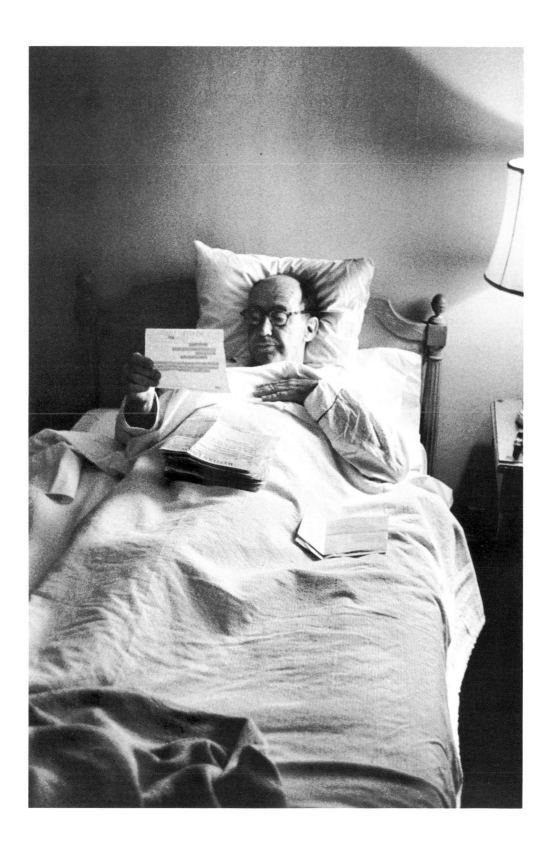

VI

ABROAD AND AT HOME

PHOTOGRAPHS BY
JOHN FELL STEVENSON

Even after his crushing defeat in 1956, Stevenson's influence in the country and abroad was still a powerful force. He went on doing enough speaking to keep him in the news, although most of the official opposition role he had played between 1952 and 1956 was taken over by a new body, the Democratic Advisory Council, formed by leading Democrats at Stevenson's suggestion in order to provide a source for organized, articulate party opposition. The council periodically issued statements and position papers that plainly showed the marks of Stevenson's thinking and example.

In the autumn of 1957, not long after Russia launched Sputnik, there came an unusual tribute to Stevenson's continuing political stature. Secretary of State John Foster Dulles wanted bipartisan national support for American policy at an important NATO meeting in Paris in December, and in order to assure it he invited Stevenson to help prepare the United States program for that meeting. Stevenson agreed to be a consultant, hoping he could persuade the administration to shift its emphasis from the military aspects of our alliances and foreign relations to the social and economic, but he was not successful. After three and a half weeks he submitted his final recommendations and did not accompany the President to Paris.

He still traveled on his own, of course. Generally he took several companions and met with national leaders wherever he went. In the summer of 1958 it was to the Soviet Union, his first visit there since 1926. He spent two hours in conversation with Khrushchev; outside of Moscow, he saw vast sections of the country normally closed to foreigners. All over Russia he found a friendliness, warmth and curiosity entirely unconnected with official Soviet propaganda.

In the early part of 1960 Stevenson spent ten weeks in South America. He came home eager to talk about what he had observed, but reporters who met him at the airport were asking not about the trip but whether he would be a candidate again in 1960.

CONVERSATION WITH KHRUSHCHEV *From Stevenson's account of their meeting in* Friends and Enemies, *published by Harper in 1959.*

Mr. Khrushchev received me for what turned out to be a wide-ranging two-and-one-half hour conversation in his long, narrow, plain office in the old Royal Palace of the Kremlin. Portraits of Marx and Lenin looked down from the dun-colored walls (in the provinces, Stalin is still looking down, too). Mr. Khrushchev is a short, stout, bald man who looks his age of sixty-four. His manner is unpretentious and jovial; his laugh is quick and infectious, and there is an unmistakable ring of authority in his low voice.☐

Our talk ranged over many subjects . . . trade between the United States and the Soviet Union, economic aid for the underdeveloped countries, the satellites, Western anxiety about Soviet objectives, etc. But always Khrushchev brought the talk back to his question: "How shall we improve our political relations?"

We found ourselves in hearty agreement on one broad general principle which should govern the conduct of the great powers: No interference in the affairs of smaller countries. But I'm afraid we were "at opposite poles" again in our ideas of what constitutes interference.

I raised, for example, the recent stern Soviet behavior toward the satellites as an illustration of why there is tension and fear in the West of Soviet intentions. Mentioning the current Soviet campaign against what is called "revisionism," and the retreat from his earlier liberal idea of "many roads to socialism," I asked why Soviet policy had grown rigid and Stalinist again. We in America, I went on, feel that all nations should have the right to go in any direction they wish, and are disturbed when we see this right interfered with, even inside the Communist world.

Mr. Khrushchev's manner hardened. He expressed surprise at my interest in ideological disputes "since the capitalists do not consider it possible to build a Communist society." But he quickly added, "No interference in the internal affairs of other countries—let us write that rule down and approve it at a summit conference. We want to establish it and hold it sacred, for these affairs should only be settled by the peoples concerned."

When I asked if that had been the Soviet Union's attitude at the time of the armed intervention in Hungary and the recent denunciation of Tito and Yugoslavia, he let me have it. Following the familiar Communist debating tactic of attack, Mr. Khrushchev assailed the United States and its actions around the world—in Lebanon, Jordan, Guatemala—even Cuba!

"The trouble is that Americans poke their noses where they shouldn't," he complained.

The question had struck a sensitive chord. "I am sure," he went on, "that neither Tito nor Kadar authorized Mr. Stevenson to raise this question. If I wrote Comrade Tito [and he emphasized the word Comrade], he would undoubtedly be deeply shocked, and all the more so would Comrade Kadar, for these are internal matters."

As for Hungary, he went on to say that he was planning to spend his summer vacation with the head of the present Hungarian government, Kadar, and would tell him about my "solicitude" for Hungary.

Then, as though expressing an afterthought, he added, "Let's go together and we will speak to the Hungarian people together and set forth our respective positions to them, and we'll see which position the people will support."

To this I had to reply, "I am afraid that the Hungarian government I am talking about cannot speak any more." And that ended our discussion on Hungary.

He ended the whole subject of the Communist bloc impatiently, "It would be better not to raise questions which relate solely to us and the foreign Communist parties. We and Tito are Communists, and somehow we will settle this affair. It is an internal affair, and in any event you couldn't help us. Let's rather talk about questions of how best to improve relations between us and the United States."

By implication at least, he was saying that whatever goes on in the Communist world is a family affair and doesn't concern outsiders, that Soviet suppression of the uprising in Hungary in 1956 was not "interference" and that Soviet pressure on Yugoslavia to conform to Moscow is not a case of meddling in another country's affairs. But he also made it clear that what happens in the non-Communist world (the "capitalist" world) *is* a proper concern of the Soviet Union. It is hard for us to believe that Russia is afraid of the United States. But I think the Soviet leaders at least really are. And certainly American security measures are uppermost among Russia's fears. "We see ourselves encircled by your bases," Mr. Khrushchev said. "There are no Soviet troops in the Near and Middle East, but the Americans have bases in England, Turkey, Greece, and I don't know where they don't have them. What would you Americans think if we set up bases in Mexico, or some such place? How would you feel?"

The policy of Mr. Dulles, he went on, is one of "rollback." "But history will roll him back. The policy of rollback must be rolled back. You cannot roll us back. On this basis there not only cannot be friendship, there cannot even be good relations."

I told Mr. Khrushchev what he knows full well—that the bases represent only a response to our fear of postwar Soviet ambitions. And, while I wanted to hear Mr. Khrushchev talk rather than myself, I thought it best to briefly put the record straight. So I also reminded him that after the war, in which we had fought Hitler as allies, we genuinely believed in continuing co-operation. We almost totally disarmed, offered to share the atomic secret with the world, gave up the Philippines and pressed hard for an effective United Nations, a work in which I was personally engaged after the war.

But then came a whole series of disillusioning events—Soviet pressure on Greece and Turkey, the coup in Czechoslovakia, the division of Germany, Soviet subjugation of all eastern Europe from the Baltic to the Black Sea, the war in Korea, arms to Egypt. I said our policy had not been aggressive or expansive, but to defend our security and the right of all countries to go their own way, unmolested and secure.

"Mr. Premier," I concluded, "there should be no conflicts between us. We each have enough territory and resources. Our troubles arise from the outside. Maybe we Americans have made mistakes, but this is the way we see things, and I'm sure that my countrymen are very eager to find a way to settle the conflicts that divide us."

"This I believe," Mr. Khrushchev answered, and paid me a pretty compliment. "I have read your speeches. Some things in them are wrong and even offensive [sounded like campaign time at home!], but on the whole I think you stand for improving relations and we welcome it." And then he went on to say something about Soviet attitudes that I think is little understood among us Americans.

He stated frankly and confidently that the world is inexorably going Communist.

"You must understand, Mr. Stevenson, that we live in an epoch when one system is giving way to another. When you established your republican system in the eighteenth century, the English didn't like it. Now, too, a process is taking place in which the peoples want to live under a new system of society; and it is necessary that one agree and reconcile himself with this fact. The process should take place without interference. If this principle [of non-interference] were accepted, it would improve the international climate and we would welcome it. But you are playing the part of a gendarme again—in the Middle East."

Thus, the prescription given me by the leader of the Soviet Union appears to be that events inside the Communist world are none of our business, but the non-Communist world must stand aside while his "new system of society" exploits the nationalist awakening and social unrest in the world, and spreads from country to country.

Perhaps I misunderstood him. I hope so, because such an outlook leaves little hope for the better relations and increasing confidence that are indispensable to peace, security and disarmament.

Moreover, he is wrong. The peoples of the small countries of eastern Europe did not choose communism; it was imposed on them by the Red Army at the end of the war. The Czech people did not want to live under that system; they were victims of a Communist coup in 1948—and the atmosphere of suppression there, as I have observed it, bears mute testimony to this fact even now, a decade after.

Communism has had its way in Europe only by force and conspiracy; not by choice. The nationalism and the social unrest in so many parts of the world aren't a Communist revolution. They are a revolt against foreign domination, feudalism and misery. And communism isn't the way to national independence either, as the Soviet satellites can testify. Moreover the new Russian Empire is a jail—you can't get out once you're in—as Hungary bears witness. Just now we live in hope that the peoples of the Middle East may not have to learn that lesson the hard way.

And I might have added that social reform was not a Soviet monopoly; that they had evidently been so busy trying to make their system work they had overlooked the vast changes in Western society—the redistribution of wealth, growth of industrial democracy and the new concepts of social responsibility. But I have a hunch they don't want to see what has happened in the West which makes so much of their Marx-Lenin bible obsolete and idiotic.

Here I must add that Khrushchev envisages the further expansion of communism as a peaceful process. No hint of war or the old fire and brimstone rhetoric ever entered the talk.

Russia is changing, too, and memories of the horror of the last war are still fresh. At all events "peace and friendship" was on every official lip and was the burden of the greeting from the good-natured crowds in public places everywhere we traveled. Khrushchev was no exception. As I have said, I would not be surprised if he was as afraid of us as we are of them. After all, economic development and improved living standards are the first priority in Russia, and the rapid progress envisioned in the seven-year plan is dependent on peace. And Khrushchev's idea of Communist expansion by non-violent means, through what he calls "competition of the two systems," may account for the new sensitivity of Soviet foreign policy to world public opinion.

Stevenson with Khrushchev at a luncheon on an Iowa farm in 1959.

OUR BROKEN MAINSPRING *From a lecture delivered in Washington, D.C.,* *January 18, 1959.*

It is impossible to spend weeks traveling around the Soviet Union, as I did this summer, without taking away an overwhelming impression of thrust and purpose in most aspects of Soviet life. The revolutionary ardor of the early days to be sure has cooled with time, but even the very pragmatic political leaders seem to believe profoundly in the truth of their way of life and are quietly confident that it will sweep the whole world in time. I think they sincerely believe that their methods, their aspirations, their dreams, make up the final truth about the nature of man and society; that collective man in the collective state is the ultimate unfolding of human destiny, the end of history, the "far-off divine event" for which mankind has been in long travail, the vision of "all things made new" that has haunted men's minds ever since Christianity thrust into human thought the intoxicating ideal of a perfected humanity.

From this conviction, if I have not overstated it, flow two consequences. The first is that no effort, no dedication, no sacrifice is too great that may help to realize the Communist party's goals in Soviet society. The second is that no corner of humanity can be a matter of indifference to the Communists, because the whole human race is destined to become in time one Communist brotherhood.

The energy, the drive, the dedication in the U.S.S.R. spill over into international affairs in ways that we are only now beginning to realize. In part, of course, this is the restless concern which all imperial powers must exercise, especially when the peoples they control are as restive and unreliable as the captive peoples in Russia's European empire. But Communist activity, planning and efforts in trade and aid are not confined to areas of Communist control. They are world-wide, and there is no corner of the earth's surface which the Russians think too insignificant for their attention, none.

All this we know—or begin to know. But I wonder how often we try to grasp the scale of dedication that lies behind it. Why should they be so busy? Why so much work and thought? Why such diversion of precious resources? Why such patience through every setback, such forward thrusts through every point of Western weakness? Heaven knows, we only want to stay home. Why don't they? Why do we never meet an isolationist Communist? These are some of the questions that haunted me when I confronted at first hand this iron, forceful, formidable way of life.

And I do not think that there is any doubt about the answer. Part of it is simply needed foreign trade. Part is fear, the search for security through friends. And part is the historical centrifugal forces in Russia which have been pressing outward for two hundred years—to the Pacific, the Balkans, the Middle East, the Straits and so on. But the important thing is that the Soviet Russians believe in their truth, as the men of the Western world once believed in theirs. They, not we, are firing the shots that are heard round the world—and also the satellites that orbit above it. The fact that their faith is in many ways an evil perversion of the great propositions that once made the blood course in Western veins does not alter the fact that their tempo is dynamic and rapid, ours sluggish—even, I think, to ourselves.

Surely, the reason cannot be that we Americans have lost our vision of truth and brotherhood. No country on earth owes the sense of community more explicitly to the fact that it is united not by race or nationality but by fidelity to an idea. We were born "dedicated to a proposition" and our greatest leaders—the Jeffersons, the Lincolns, the Wilsons—were not great because they achieved purely American purposes, but because they were able to speak for humanity at large and extend their vision to the whole family of man.

Nor, I believe, can we find fault with the substance of what we have endearingly called the American dream. Its truths are still "self-evident." The possession of liberty and the pursuit of happiness—rightly understood—these have not been overthrown as the highest goods of human society. Indeed, the ferment of our freedom works inexorably and dangerously in the Communist world. No one can have visited Poland without seeing how little the Polish people really accept their servitude and how they look beyond their neighbors to the free world as the reservoir of power and of hope.

But, alas, on the basis of the record, one would hardly suspect that the Western world possessed so powerful a weapon. Our talk—in diplomacy, in strategy, in aid and trade, in all of the intricacies of our world-wide relations—has been to a depressing degree purely defensive. We have offered aid not to help others but to shield ourselves. We have reacted to countless Soviet initiatives; acted on our own initiative barely at all. We watch the skies for other people's Sputniks and listen to the telegraph wires for other people's moves. Yet we are the free men of this universe; we are the children of liberty, the beneficiaries of unequaled abundance and heirs of the highest, proudest political tradition ever known to man!

Why this lack of initiative? Why this paralysis of will? What have we done to our truth, our brotherhood—the supreme truth of freedom, the Christian truth of brotherly love? Have they failed? Or have we?

There is no more urgent duty than to discover why we have failed, if we have, and I think we have, and to get back into the arena, aspiring, striving, fighting, if you please, once more for what we believe. An examination of what you might call our collective conscience is to my mind far more important than particular projects or programs. You can have a perfect assembly of pieces in your watch, but they are worthless if the mainspring is broken. I am not worried about our various pieces—our technology, our science, our machines, our resources. But I am concerned, desperately concerned, about our mainspring. That it has run down, we know. But is it broken; is it broken beyond repair? In the last analysis, no question is worth more consideration in America today.

And I would like to suggest some of the ways in which it seems to me we have enfeebled the great central pulse of our freedom, the great truth of liberty,

Stevenson with Russian Orthodox leaders in Zagorsk during the summer of 1958.

which, more than any other nation, we first set working in the modern world.

Goethe, who also lived through a crisis of freedom, said to his generation: "What you have inherited from your fathers, earn over again for yourselves or it will not be yours." We inherited this freedom we talk about so glibly. We seem unaware that it has to be remade and re-earned in each generation of man. One reason for this failure is, I believe, passing at last. In recent years we were stifled with complacent self-confidence. We believed ourselves dominant in every field. We talked of "the American Century." We forgot the ardors and the efforts that had given us a measure of pre-eminence. Complacency made us impervious to ideas, even the obvious idea that we are in danger. So we assumed that all we needed was to sit still and enjoy the "peace and prosperity" that was our right.

I believe that phase is now passing. Our foolish languor has been shaken, if not shattered. We are more ready to examine ourselves and our record. And it is a privilege of our society that every citizen should make his own inquiry. If I stress one or the other aspect of the problem, this is simply my angle of vision. You will have yours. The urgent thing is to feel the need for re-thinking and to set to work the ultimate energies of a free society—which cannot be done by the fiat of government but only by the troubled conscience of responsible men and women.

I believe—as I have said before—that we have confused the free with the free and easy. If freedom had been the happy, simple, relaxed state of ordinary humanity, man would have everywhere been free—whereas through most of time and space he has been in chains. Do not let us make any mistake about this. The natural government of man is servitude. Tyranny is the normal pattern of government. It is only by intense thought, by great effort, by burning idealism and unlimited sacrifice that freedom has prevailed as a system of government. And the efforts which were first necessary to create it are fully as necessary to sustain it in our own day.

He who offers this thing that we call freedom as the soft option is a deceiver or himself deceived. He who sells it cheap or offers it as the by-product of this or that economic system is knave or fool. For freedom demands infinitely more care and devotion than any other political system. It puts consent and personal initiative in the place of command and obedience. By relying upon the devotion and initiative of ordinary citizens, it gives up the harsh but effective disciplines that underpin all the tyrannies which over the millennia have stunted the full stature of man.

But of what use is escape from external restraint if given the opportunity man simply stunts himself? If freedom means ease alone, if it means shirking the hard disciplines of learning, if it means evading the rigors and rewards of creative activity, if it means more expenditure on advertising than on education, if it means "bachelor cooking" and "life adjustment" courses in the schools, and the steady cult of the trivial and the mediocre, if it means—worst of all—indifference, even contempt for all but athletic excellence in our educational system, we may keep for a time the forms of free society, but its spirit will be dead.

I believe we have had enough of adjustment, of conformity, of easy options and the least common denominator in our system. We need instead to see the "pursuit of happiness" in terms which are historically proven and psychologically correct. The dreary failure in history of all classes committed to pleasure and profit alone, the vacuity and misery accompanying the sole pursuit of ease—the collapse of the French aristocracy, the corruption of imperial Rome, the decline and fall of the resplendent Manchus—all these facts of history do not lose their point because the pleasures of today are mass pleasures and no longer the enjoyments of an elite. If we become a nation of Bourbons, numbers will not save us. We shall go their way, too. Vacuity and indifference are not redeemed by the fact that everyone can share in them. They merely restrict the circle from which regeneration can come.

I say this—I hope you will believe me—in no Puritan or pleasure-hating spirit. On the contrary, there is no boredom, no misery to equal the pursuit of distraction alone. We do not slip into happiness. It is strenuously sought and earned. A nation glued to recreation, to the television screen, is not simply at a loss before the iron pioneers of the new collective society. It is not even having a good time. No society has ever spent as much as we do on drink and tranquilizers. Can one argue that this is evidence of universal fun? I ran across a quotation from La Bruyère on the court of Louis XIV which struck me as relevant: "Les joies sont visibles, mais fausses, et les chagrins cachés, mais réels"—its joys are visible, but artificial, and its sorrows hidden, but real.

But perhaps this misunderstanding of the true nature of happiness and of the conditions of its pursuit is simply an aspect of something else—our misunderstanding of the real nature of freedom. I recall the words of the wise Judge Learned Hand, who warned us that freedom would not survive in our Constitution if it had already died in the hearts of the people. We shall not have a free society unless we have free men.

And how often do we reflect upon what this inner freedom entails? "Give me the man," cries Hamlet, "who is not passion's slave." But this is what we are in danger of becoming, slaves to a tyranny more intimate and inescapable than any that Stalin or Mao Tse-tung could impose. We can be made slaves simply by the clutter and complexity of modern living—which notoriously leaves no time for serious thought and offers every means of distraction so that we can avoid such thought. Between aircraft that take us everywhere more rapidly, newspapers that grow in weight and coverage, news that flashes round the globe, ceaseless and competitive entertainment, fashions—God help us! that—change from sack to trapeze and back again, we can fill up every "unforgiving minute" with enough trash and preoccupation to still forever the deeper voices of the soul. Like Matthew Arnold, we can

> ". . . see all sights from pole to pole,
> And glance and nod and hustle by,
> And never once possess our soul
> Before we die."

How are we to defend freedom if for the tyranny of external control we substitute the clattering, cluttering tyranny of internal aimlessness and fuss? This freedom of our souls, freedom at the profoundest level of our being, is not a gift to us by our contemporary way of life. On the contrary, much of this life is a direct conspiracy against it. And if we cannot—by a certain discipline, by readiness for reflection and quiet, by determination to do the difficult and aim at a lasting good—rediscover the real purpose and direction of our existence, we shall not be free. Our society will not be free. And between a chaotic, selfish, indifferent, commercial society and the iron discipline of the Communist world, I would not like to predict the outcome. Outer tyranny with purpose may well triumph over the inner, purposeless tyranny of a confused and aimless way of life.

I doubt if any society in history has faced so great a moral challenge as ours, or needed more desperately to draw on the deepest sources of courage and responsibility. Ours is the first human community in which resources are so abundant that almost no policies lie beyond our capacity for purely physical reasons. What we decide to do, we can do. The inhibitions of poverty—lack of resources, lack of capital, lack of power—do not hold us back. We can accomplish what we aim at. Thus, perhaps for the first time in the world, choice, not means, ends, not instruments, are decisive.

Then again we have proved—drably and dangerously—over the last decade that defensiveness is not a sufficient reason for action. All the policies we have pursued in self-defense have left us still on the defensive. But if we do not act from fear, we must find some other motivation. In free society there is no other alternative but to tap the vigor, the faith, the imagination of the people themselves. We must find out once more who we are, as the psychologists say.

But perhaps the most urgent reason why the quality of our moral response has become the decisive issue in politics is quite simply that most of the major problems of our day present themselves in moral terms, and are probably insoluble without some stirring of generosity, some measure of vision. Let me give you three instances. In the wealthiest nation in the world, at least five million families still live in squalid but remediable poverty. They are a minority. They do not have the votes to force the issue of their misfortune into the front rank of public issues. They depend, for remedies, upon the alert conscience of the majority. But how do we keep the conscience sensitive and alert? By concentrating on our own concerns? By adding the dishwasher to the television set to the air conditioner? By griping over taxes and attacking that great bogey we call "the welfare state"? By closing our minds every time our shiny car takes us through a slum? No—we shall have the dedication, the drive to wipe poverty out of this rich land only if the well-to-do majority of today do not repeat the selfish indifference which, in many communities, has been the epitaph of the well-to-do of yesterday.

Or take the issue of the rights and status of our colored citizens. This is our small share of a world-wide problem. The four hundred years of dominance of men of white skin is ending. The vast colored majority of mankind are seeking the opportunity and the respect which white people have been lucky enough to enjoy for so long—sometimes at the colored people's expense. But within this world-wide crisis we in America, with our colored minority, have a major role to play—for good or evil. "The unfinished work" which Lincoln left us, of creating a society in which all men can hold up their heads as equals and self-respecting citizens, can never be accomplished unless there are enough white men and women who resist to the core of their being the moral evil of treating any of God's children as essentially inferior.

Nor is this simply a question of our own national community. I come back to the painful fact that the Communists show a world-wide concern which is largely lacking among the men of the West. The whole human race is their horizon. Their "brotherhood" is materialist, collectivist, atheist, and we dislike it, but it embraces everybody, and it is the framework of policies which take the missionaries of their new order to the ends of the earth. I say with all the emphasis that I can command that we have no corresponding commitment to our fellow man. For hundreds of years, we have preached the Christian promise of brotherhood, but today, when vanishing space and scientific revolution have turned our planet into a single neighborhood, the ideal means little in terms of concern or conviction, in terms of policy or of action.

Here we are in the Atlantic world, 16 per cent of the world's peoples consuming 70 per cent of the world's wealth. We cannot be indifferent to the moral implications of this gigantic gap. I do not know how we can gain a new perspective about the narrow world of plenty and of poverty in which we live unless moral insights of justice and compassion stir us to understand the privileged position in which we live.

We are not going to be stirred to action by our own needs. We are the cushioned, the protected, the fortunate minority. It is not the measure of our morals or the lesson of our history to be spurred on only by fear of Russian encroachment. What we have done has largely been from this motivation, and it has left us on the defensive. Our hope is to accept the implications of our own faith, to make concrete the image of brotherhood which we profess, to set to work to express our dedication in whatever effort or sacrifice the world's needs may dictate. And, if we must always think in terms of contest with the Soviets, let us bear in mind that the ability to create the good life for the greatest numbers will be decisive.

This age has been defined in many ways—as a time of conflict in ideology, as a time of ferment in technology, as a period of revolution in science, as an era when at last the means lie at hand to free mankind from the ancient shackles of pain and hunger. It is all these things—but I believe the true crisis of our time lies at a deeper level. We have indeed conquered means and resources unknown at earlier ages. We have had thrown open to us frontiers of choice which would have left earlier ages stupefied by their scale and their scope.

But all this freedom and elbow room only thrusts onto us with more force the fundamental issue of the truth that is within us. We can use our wealth, our capacity for some vision of truth, some ideal of brotherhood, or we can imprison ourselves within the selfishness of our own concerns and the limitations of a narrow nationhood. This is the dimension of our crisis.

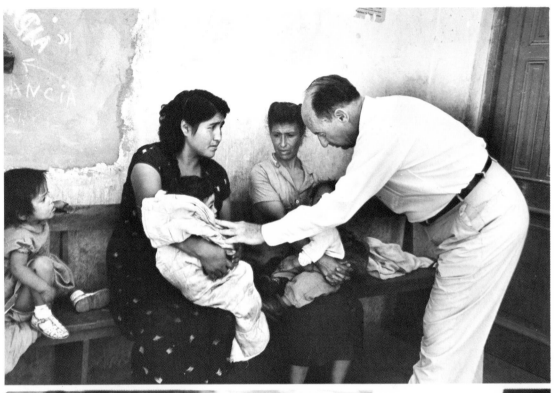

Stevenson talking to a state delegation at the 1960 convention in Los Angeles. With him are his son Adlai III and daughter-in-law Nancy.

VII

LOS ANGELES: 1960

Just after the election in 1956, Stevenson said publicly and without any qualifying phrases, "I shall not again be a candidate." As 1960 approached, more and more people refused to take his no as a final answer. His own position never changed. "I am not a candidate," he said again and again. But he endorsed no one else, and his supporters put together a dedicated organization based on the hope that at the convention a dead-lock would develop among Kennedy, Symington and Johnson, and that Stevenson was the only man strong enough to emerge the winner in such circumstances. Stevenson himself, until the end, continually refused to say that he would accept a draft, but he just as scrupulously did not say that he would refuse one.

As the Los Angeles convention opened, nomination seemed virtually in the hands of Senator Kennedy already, but Stevenson's partisans were undaunted. When he made his first appearance on the floor as a delegate from Illinois, the crowds cheered for ten minutes without interruption. This demonstration was only a mild preamble to what came three nights later when Senator Eugene McCarthy of Minnesota rose and in an eloquent speech nominated Adlai Stevenson. As McCarthy finished, the galleries burst into pandemonium, which no one could bring under control for twenty-five minutes. A gigantic papier-mâché ball bearing the legend "Draft Stevenson" appeared; banners and placards waved; tumult prevailed. But the noise rose from the galleries, not the delegates. When the nomination came to a vote, Kennedy's beautifully organized campaign brought him victory on the first ballot.

GOOD-BYE, NOT FAREWELL *A statement Stevenson made on July 15, 1960, the day after John F. Kennedy won the Democratic nomination.*

I have come to say good-bye—but not farewell.

This is not the end of a journey. It is a beginning—a new and splendid beginning for the Democratic party and for America. And it is my privilege to present the leader of that new beginning, chosen here in Los Angeles in accordance with the time tested practice of the oldest political organization on earth—the Democratic party. Far and wide, people struggling to plant the tender seeds of democracy have witnessed the stirring drama enacted here in Los Angeles. They have seen how our party system works. And they have noted how yesterday's competition for party leadership becomes today's solidarity for party victory.

Twice I have been the beneficiary of this last and glorious hour of the nominating process of the Democratic party. And twice my spirit has been enriched by the confidence of millions of Americans. But the spontaneous outpouring of labor, loyalty and love all across the country in the past few weeks and, finally, here in Los Angeles has been the most enriching experience of my life.

I have no words to express my thanks; but I do have words to express my hopes—my hope that all of you who have lifted my heart will share my enthusiasm for this new beginning for the Democratic party and for our country; my hope that every one of you will join me in making this new beginning a reality in the election next November.

For too long our nation has been groping in a mist of uncertain values. Now, at last, we have the promise of deliverance, the promise of a return to the realities of our times, the promise of the clarity of direction and the magnanimity of purpose which have illuminated America's proudest hours.

We have spoken at the convention our disquiet, our distress about the place of America today in the eyes and minds and hearts of the world. These years of quiet drift have been years of quiet decline. Softly our country has slipped ever closer to national peril.

Even through the din and clamor of the convention we have been dimly aware of new crises in the Congo and in Cuba, new turbulence in the world, new threats from the Kremlin. Let no one think that this rush of trouble is purely a natural calamity, beyond our control and beyond our responsibility. Many things are indeed beyond our control, but many more are the direct product of our own unwillingness to identify and confront the hazards of this revolutionary age. The headlines of today are the heritage of yesterday. They are angry symptoms which our nation dare no longer ignore, from which we can no longer avert our eyes. The time is long overdue, not alone for searching self-examination, but for prompt, bold action.

But to declare our ideals of equality, of justice, of peace is not to achieve them; that has been the tragic error of this epoch of illusion. To achieve an ideal is to face the hard actuality of choice and to conquer the hard necessity of decision.

We rejoice that we no longer have to argue with the Republicans over the great social reforms which we used to call the New Deal. And we rejoice, even more, that internationalism and the principle of collective security in this shrinking world is no longer a partisan dispute in America.

But we still see children growing up in slums, we still see children jammed into stifling classrooms, we still see older people whose needs go unmet, we still see some among us who are denied their birthright because of their race. And we still see peace and the survival of our ideals of freedom and justice and order in the world more elusive than ever, after these listless, comfortable years of illusion.

Revitalizing our purposes, resuming our responsibility in the world, will demand great strength of arm, of head, of heart. But our nation cannot rest—our people will not rest—on the march toward that distant day where no one rattles a saber, where all dwell without fear, where the struggle is not to frighten and to enslave men, but to liberate their decency and to vindicate their dignity.

Just eight years ago on a similar occasion I said: ". . . more important than winning the election is governing the nation. That is the test of a political party— the acid, final test. When the tumult and the shouting die, when the bands are gone and the lights are dimmed, there is the stark reality of responsibility in an hour of history haunted with those gaunt, grim specters of strife, dissension and materialism at home, and ruthless, inscrutable and hostile power abroad."

Tonight the world is darker, the task of governing even greater. But with "realism and responsibility" for our motto, America will become again what we once were, the guiding star of the hopes of free men. The moments of American greatness have been those when its leaders have awakened the strength that lies in no one man, in no government, but in people.

President Kennedy and Ambassador Stevenson in the President's White House office, February 1961.

VIII

AT THE UNITED NATIONS

PHOTOGRAPHS BY
INGE MORATH

When Kennedy was elected, people speculated that he would make Stevenson his Secretary of State, and there is no doubt that Stevenson wanted the job. But Kennedy was not under any obligation to Stevenson, who had not supported him at the convention. In December the new President-elect offered Stevenson the job of Ambassador to the United Nations—and an elevation of that position to cabinet rank, so that Stevenson could have a voice in making the policy he would have to defend and carry out. Stevenson accepted. His appointment was widely considered to underline the new administration's high opinion of the United Nations and its stress of that body as a forum for foreign policy.

Stevenson assumed his duties in New York at the end of January 1961, in the midst of the agonizing Congo crisis. His arrival was greeted warmly. But less than three months later he suffered an embarrassment severely compromising to him. During the invasion of the Bay of Pigs in Cuba, Stevenson was kept in ignorance of any American participation, and he hotly defended his country's innocence. With his own personal integrity on the line in this defense, his position was suddenly exposed when President Kennedy publicly accepted responsibility for the disaster. Stevenson felt his effectiveness as ambassador had been greatly reduced but that this moment of crisis would be a terrible time for him to quit his post. He elected to continue, with Kennedy's assurance that in the future no major policy decisions would be made without him. In June the President sent Stevenson on an important tour of Latin America in an attempt to repair the severe damage done to the United States' reputation in the Bay of Pigs fiasco.

After that, respect for Stevenson at the United Nations grew stronger all the time. He weathered extraordinary crises there—the continuing problems in the Congo, the discovery of Russian missile bases in Cuba, the death of Dag Hammarskjöld, the assassination of President Kennedy, and the personal shock and loss he felt when Eleanor Roosevelt died. In the first half of 1965, he was caught up in the trying problem of how to hold the United Nations General Assembly together when some of its members, particularly the Soviet Union, refused to pay dues for peace-keeping operations of which they disapproved.

In July 1965, on a trip back from Geneva, Stevenson stopped for a few days in London. On the warm afternoon of July 14, as he was walking down a London street, he collapsed of a heart attack and was dead.

THE CONGO CRISIS *From a statement to the Security Council, February 15, 1961, only two weeks after Stevenson had made his first official appearance at the United Nations.*

We regret that the Soviet government has not as yet seen fit to cooperate with states which truly seek peace in attempting to work out constructive steps for the solution of the agonizing problems the Congolese people are now facing. Instead, the Soviet government proposes the complete abandonment of the United Nations operation in the Congo. And in one month!

What does this mean? It means, my colleagues, not only the abandonment of the Congo to chaos and to civil war—to, if you please, the cold war—it means abandonment of the principle of the United Nations itself.

Does any one doubt it would mean chaos? Does this Council, the *Security* Council, favor abandoning security for insecurity and anarchy?

Do we want to withdraw the only elements that stand foursquare against civil and tribal war? Does the Soviet government really want Africans to kill Africans? The United States does not, and it devoutly hopes that the Soviet government does not, too, and that it will join the United States and other peace-loving states in supporting and strengthening the only force that can prevent Congolese civil war—the United Nations.

And now the cold war. Does the Soviet government really want to chill what should be warm and temperate in Africa with the icy blasts of power politics? The United States does not. Its only interest in the Congo is to support the Congolese people in their struggle for real independence, free from any foreign domination from *any* source.

The United States deplores any war, cold or otherwise. Its only desire is to live in peace and freedom and to let all other peoples live in peace and freedom. It will resist with all of its power all assaults on its own peace and freedom, and it proposes to join with all other peace-loving peoples in resisting, in the cooperative framework of the United Nations, all assaults on the peace and freedom of other peoples.

In that spirit, we declare that—so far as we are concerned—Africa shall never be the scene of any war, cold or hot. But we also declare that Africa for the Africans *means* Africa for the Africans, and not Africa as a hunting ground for alien ambitions. And we pledge our full and unstinted support against any attempt by anyone to interfere with the full and free development by Africans of their own independent African future.

We believe that the only way to keep the cold war *out* of the Congo is to keep the United Nations *in* the Congo, and we call on the Soviet Union to join us in thus ensuring the free and untrammeled exercise by the Congolese people of their right to independence and to democracy. □

The United Nations has not achieved perfection, nor has the United States, and they probably never will. The United States, like the United Nations, is composed of humans; it has made mistakes, it probably always will make mistakes; it has never pleased all people, it cannot please all people; in its desire and whole-hearted determination to do justice, it may offend one group of states in 1952, another in 1956 and perhaps still another in 1961. But, always, the United States has tried, and we believe it will always try, to apply even-handedly the rules of justice and equity that should govern us all.

Are we callously to cast aside the one and only instrument that men have developed to safeguard their peace and security? Are we to abandon the jungles of the Congo to the jungles of internecine warfare and internal rivalry?

The issue, then, is simply this: Shall the United Nations survive? Shall the attempt to bring about peace by the concerted power of international understand-

Stevenson with Secretary General Dag Hammarskjöld in the Security Council of the United Nations in New York.

ing be discarded? Shall any pretense of an international order, of international law, be swept aside? Shall conflicts of naked power, awful in their potential, be permitted to rage in Africa or elsewhere, unchecked by international cooperation or authority?

These are questions which call for an answer, not so much by the great powers as by the smaller ones and the newer ones. My own country, as it happens, is in the fortunate position of being able to look out for itself and for its interests, and look out it will. But it is for the vast majority of states that the United Nations has vital meaning and is of vital necessity. I call on those states to rise in defense of the integrity of the institution which is, for them, the only assurance of their freedom and their liberty, and the only assurance for all of us of peace in the years to come.

THE GREATEST OF HUMAN UNDERTAKINGS *Stevenson's opinion of the United Nations was always high. This is the text of a broadcast he made during his first Presidential campaign, on October 24, 1952.*

We do more today than to observe the anniversary of an institution. What we do today is to hold communion with an idea.

I speak of the idea of peace on earth.

The pursuit of this idea is at once old and new. It is as old as man's discovery that he could conquer and enslave other men. In the same sense, it is as old as the will to resist, as old as the power of a righteous cause. But it is also a young idea, this pursuit of peace, for it is only in our century that human wisdom and energy have sought to bring all the nations of the earth under a rule of law through world organization.

If the pursuit of peace is both old and new, it is also both complicated and simple. It is complicated, for it has to do with people, and nothing in this universe baffles man as much as man himself. Much of nature's mystery has come under man's mastery. Heat, cold, wind and rain have lost their terrors, but the environment man has created for himself has yet to be brought under control. Nature's jungle has been conquered, but man still lives in the larger jungle of his fears.

Yes, it is complicated, this pursuit of peace, but there is also an inspiring simplicity to it. We can win the war against war because we must. Progress is what happens when impossibility yields to necessity. And it is an article of the democratic faith that progress is a basic law of life.

If I thought that the human race was no longer capable of human progress, I would not be trespassing now upon the time and attention of the American people. Instead, I might be off on a remote hilltop silently contemplating the closing scene of the final act of the human comedy.

But I do not believe it is man's destiny to compress this once boundless earth into a small neighborhood the better to destroy it. Nor do I believe it is in the nature of man to strike eternally at the image of himself, and therefore of God. I profoundly believe that there is on this horizon, as yet only dimly perceived, a new dawn of conscience. In that purer light, people will come to see themselves in each other, which is to say they will make themselves known to one another by their similarities rather than by their differences. Man's knowledge of things will begin to be matched by man's knowledge of self. The significance of a smaller world will be measured not in terms of military advantage, but in terms of advantage for the human community. It will be the triumph of the heartbeat over the drumbeat.

These are my beliefs and I hold them deeply, but they would be without any inner meaning for me unless I felt that they were also the deep beliefs of human beings everywhere. And the proof of this, to my mind, is the very existence of the United Nations. However great the assaults on the peace may have been since the United Nations was founded, the easiest way to demonstrate the idea behind it is by the fact that no nation in the world today would dare to remove itself from membership and separate his country from the human hopes that are woven into the very texture of the organization.

The early years of the United Nations have been difficult ones, but what did we expect? That peace would drift down from the skies like soft snow? That there would be no ordeal, no anguish, no testing, in this greatest of all human undertakings?

Any great institution or idea must suffer its pains of birth and growth. We will not lose faith in the United Nations. We see it as a living thing, and we will work and pray for its full growth and development. We want it to become what it was intended to be—a world society of nations under law; not merely law backed by force, but law backed by justice and popular consent. We believe the answer to world war can only be world law. This is our hope and our commitment, and that is why I join all Americans on this anniversary in saying: "More power to the United Nations."

OUR MEMBERSHIP IN THE U.N. *From a statement March 13, 1963, to the United States Senate Subcommittee on Foreign Relations.*

To form mature judgments as to the real value of the United Nations to the interests of the United States, it seems to me that we must raise alternatives, that we must ask questions which challenge the imagination to say what might have happened if the United Nations had not been there at all. For example:

Would the Communists have fared better or worse in their efforts to divert the independence movement into a Communist mold—their supreme opportunity to extend power—if the United Nations had not existed?

Would the prospects of peace be better or worse—in Iran, in Greece, in Korea, in Kashmir, in the Middle East, in the Western Pacific, in Central Africa —if there had been no United Nations during the past decade and a half?

Would United States foreign policy interests more recently in the Congo and the Caribbean have been served better or worse without a United Nations?

Could the United States put its ideas, its beliefs, its policies before the watching world more—or less—effectively if the United Nations did not exist?

I shall not attempt to speculate on these rather frightening alternatives for, it seems to me, the questions answer themselves.

But I should like to conclude with a few comments about the position of those who favor the United Nations, in principle, but want to withdraw or restrict our support on those relatively few occasions when the United States finds itself in a minority position.

The basic point here, of course, is that the United States does not own or control the United Nations. It is not a wing of the State Department. We are no more and no less than the most influential of the 110 members. If we were less, we would be failing to exert the influence of freedom's leader; if we were more, we would destroy the effectiveness of the United Nations, which depends precisely on the fact that it is not an arm of the United States, or of any other government, but a truly international organization, no better or worse than the agreements which can be reached by the controlling majorities of its members.

Before such agreements are reached—or not reached—debate and negotiation bare differences and reveal similarities which frequently lead to accommodation and compromise. And I would ask: Is this not the heart of the democratic method? Is this not the parliamentary system in action? Is this not our own idea of how we are most likely to make more wise decisions than foolish ones, how the weak are most likely to be protected from the strong, how the will of the majority and the rights of the minority can both find expression without injustice to either?

The answer to these questions is yes. And, if we were to pick up our marbles and go home whenever there is a disappointment, we would not only destroy the effectiveness of the United Nations, but would abandon hope that nations can work out their problems most of the time by the same methods by which conflicting interests get resolved within democratic nations and communities. This would deny—on the international level—the principles, methods and techniques which we swear by on the national and local levels.

Even faith in our kind of institutions would not, however, be enough to justify support for the United Nations if it worked against us. But this dilemma, happily, does not exist, and the record proves it. The fact is that the story of the last General Assembly, when the United States position was the majority position better than four times out of five, is the standard story of succeeding Assemblies over the past seventeen years. The fact is that, in seventeen years, the Soviet Union has never once—never once—succeeded in building a majority for any proposition of substance against the opposition of the United States. And the fact is that, in seventeen years, the United States has never felt obliged to exercise its veto in the Security Council to protect its interest, and the Soviet Union has used the veto a hundred times.

That's the record and there is, of course, a fundamental reason for it. The reason should be recalled frequently, for in this fact lies one of our greatest assets in the world today: The fact that the foreign policy interests of the United States

The ambassador with four of his advisors in the United Nations General Assembly.

are generally in harmony with the foreign policy interests of all nations which want to see a peaceful community of independent states working together, by free choice, to improve the lot of humanity. And since the majority of the nations of the world shares this goal, the majority consistently sides with the United States—or we side with them, depending on your point of view—when the roll is called and the yeas and nays are counted. It's as simple as that.

But let us take a couple of blemishes in the record and the performance of the United Nations and its members; the kind of blemishes that lead some of our people who favor the United Nations, in principle, to want to restrict it in practice.

First, take a case where the United States could not agree with a majority of the decision-making group in a United Nations agency. A recent case was that of the decision of the United Nations Special Fund to help finance an agricultural research project in Cuba. We objected to that project and still do. Yet the whole story is that, out of 288 projects assisted by that fund in the course of its existence, we approved of 287. So we face a choice: Should we retaliate by withholding or limiting our support for an agency which we invented, which has allocated 97 per cent of its funds to nations which we ourselves are aiding, and which represents an economical way for the United States to contribute to the Decade of Development, because in one instance out of 288 instances we were unable to persuade a majority that our view was the correct one?

Let me refer also to a situation which seems to agitate some of our people— the fact that the Soviet Union does not make the voluntary contributions which it is well able to make to such programs as technical assistance, the malaria eradication, the world food program and so forth. Their delinquency is deplorable but understandable from their point of view. These programs do not serve Communist ends; on the contrary. So it is hardly surprising that the Soviet Union makes little or no voluntary contributions to agencies whose work cuts straight across their own objectives. But should we support these programs less because they fail to win applause from the Kremlin?

As a matter of fact, I rather suspect that the Soviet Union and other Communist countries will tend to participate—and contribute—somewhat more in the work of these agencies in the years to come. There is some evidence of that already. And I think that the reason is clear. The policy of self-ostracism from the specialized agencies has not worked well for the Soviet Union, even though it has made life with them a bit easier for us.

If this in fact happens, it will raise some day-to-day problems for us; but, in my view, it also will raise problems for them and opportunities for us. For while the so-called Communist states operate more or less closed societies at home, once they step out into a United Nations forum, they enter an open society.

In an open forum, over a period of time, ideology becomes transparent, dogma wears thin and becomes tiresome and the myth of the magical solution evaporates slowly in the free air of a market place of ideas. There is contention in all this; there is frustration and the stuff of headlines; there is danger that the fearful and the insecure will want to withdraw from the free interplay of conflicting ideas and concepts and terminology, especially if, now and again, things do not go exactly the way we would like them to.

Yet it is we who do best in the open forum, for this is our natural habitat. And if we have the nerve to go ahead, if we have the stomach for the test of the open society, if we have the courage to build even that which is not perfect from our point of view, I can foresee nothing but a more meaningful dialogue coming out of it, a gradual erosion of tension, and finally the dominance of a set of ideas which are better, and better able also to stand the test, than the Marxist ideas as revealed to his successors.

All this would require, on our part, a degree of responsibility, of restraint, of maturity and of political sophistication which never before has been demanded of a democratic public and its elected representatives. It will not be easy and it will not be without temporary disappointments; and I, for one, have no doubt of the outcome, for this, too, would serve and serve well the foreign policy interests of the United States of America.

END NUCLEAR TESTING *From a statement to the Political Committee of the United Nations, October 19, 1961.*

An emergency confronts this committee and the world! The Soviet Union is now nearing the conclusion of a massive series of nuclear weapon tests. Unless something is done quickly, the Soviet testing will necessarily result in further testing by my country and perhaps by others.

There is still time to halt this drift toward the further refinement and multiplication of these weapons. Perhaps this will be the last clear chance to reverse this tragic trend. For if testing is stopped, the terrible pace of technological progress will be decisively retarded. A ban on tests is, of course, only the first step; and the control and destruction of nuclear and thermonuclear weapons is the ultimate goal. But it is an indispensable first step.

Accordingly, I must inform the committee that the United States is obliged in self-protection to reserve the right to make preparations to test in the atmosphere, as well as underground.

But the United States stands ready to resume negotiations for a treaty tomorrow. We will devote all our energies to the quickest possible conclusion of these negotiations, either here or in Geneva. If the Soviet Union will do the same and stop its tests, there is no reason why a treaty with effective controls cannot be signed in thirty days and this suicidal business ended before it ends us.

But, I repeat, unless a treaty can be signed, and signed promptly, the United States has no choice but to prepare and take the action necessary to protect its own security and that of the world community.

I trust that this expression of hope for the triumph of reason will convey some measure of the depth of our feeling about the subject and of our desire to do our share to save the human race from a greater menace than the plagues which once ravaged Europe. We believe we have done our share, and more, ever since the

United States proposals of 1946. I remind you that if those proposals had been accepted by the Soviet Union, no state would now have nuclear weapons; and we would not now be in such a perilous crisis.

I have claimed the privilege of making this declaration for the United States because few delegates, I dare say, feel more deeply about this matter than I do, in part, perhaps, because I proposed that nuclear tests be stopped almost six years ago—and lost a great many votes in the 1956 Presidential election as a result! Had the nuclear powers agreed even then, think how much safer and healthier the world would be today.

I pray we do not lose still another chance to meet the challenge of our times and stop this dance of death.

I confess a feeling of futility when I consider the immensity of the problems which confront us and the feebleness of our efforts to deal properly with them. We have lived for sixteen years in the Atomic Age. During these years we have ingeniously and steadily improved man's capacity to blow up the planet. But we have done little to improve man's control over the means of his own destruction. Instead, we have worried and wrangled and talked and trifled while time trickles away and the hands of the clock creep toward midnight.

I would not imply that the problems of control are easy. Just as the nuclear bomb itself lays open the inner mysteries of science, so the attempt to control the nuclear bomb cuts to the core of our political ideas and mechanisms. As the bomb itself represented a revolution in science, so the control of the bomb may, in the end, mean a revolution in politics.

But we must not let the very immensity of the problem dwarf our minds and our calculations. We must act—and we must take hold of the problem where we can. One obvious way is to tackle the question of nuclear testing.

No one would argue that the abolition of testing would itself solve all our problems. It would mean only a small beginning in the assault on the evil, ancient institution of war. But in a world of no beginnings, a small beginning shines forth like the morning sun on the distant horizon. We have talked long enough about the horror which hangs over us. Now is the time for us to get down to business—to fight this horror, not with soft words and wistful hopes, but with the hard weapon of effective international arrangements.

THE CUBA MISSILE CRISIS *From a statement to the Security Council, October 25, 1962.*

I want to say to you, Mr. Zorin, that I do not have your talent for obfuscation, for distortion, for confusing language and for double-talk. And I must confess to you that I am glad that I do not!

But if I understood what you said, it was that my position had changed, that today I was defensive because we did not have the evidence to prove our assertions that your government had installed long-range missiles in Cuba.

Well, let me say something to you, Mr. Ambassador—we do have the

TOP: *Stevenson in the General Assembly with his advisors.*

BOTTOM: *At a party given for Stevenson by members of the delegation from Nigeria.*

evidence. We have it, and it is clear and it is incontrovertible. And let me say something else—those weapons must be taken out of Cuba!

Next, if I understood you, you said—with a trespass on credibility that excels your best—that our position had changed since I spoke here the other day because of the pressures of world opinion and the majority of the United Nations. Well, let me say to you, sir—you are wrong again. We have had no pressure from anyone whatsoever. We came here today to indicate our willingness to discuss U Thant's proposals, and that is the only change that has taken place.

But let me also say to you, sir, that there *has* been a change. You—the Soviet Union *has* sent these weapons to Cuba. You—the Soviet Union *has* upset the balance of power in the world. You—the Soviet Union *has* created this new danger, not the United States.

And you ask, with a fine show of indignation, why the President did not tell Mr. Gromyko on last Thursday about our evidence, at the very time that Mr. Gromyko was blandly denying to the President that the U.S.S.R. was placing such weapons on sites in the New World.

Well, I will tell you why—because we were assembling the evidence, and perhaps it would be instructive to the world to see how far a Soviet official would go in perfidy. Perhaps we wanted to know if this country faced another example of nuclear deceit like that one a year ago when, in stealth, the Soviet Union broke the nuclear test moratorium.

And while we are asking questions, let me ask you why your government, your Foreign Minister, deliberately, cynically deceived us about the nuclear build-up in Cuba?

And, finally, the other day, Mr. Zorin, I remind you that you did not deny the existence of these weapons. Instead, we heard that they had suddenly become *defensive* weapons. But today, again, if I heard you correctly, you now say, with another fine flood of rhetorical scorn, they do not exist, or that we haven't proved they exist.

All right, sir, let me ask you one simple question: Do you, Ambassador Zorin, deny that the U.S.S.R. has placed and is placing medium and intermediate-range missiles and sites in Cuba? Yes or no? Don't wait for the translation. Yes or no?

[*Ambassador Zorin refused to answer, saying that he was "not in an American courtroom."*]

You are in the courtroom of world opinion. You have denied they exist, and I want to know if I understood you correctly.

I am prepared to wait for my answer until hell freezes over, if that's your decision. And I am also prepared to present the evidence in this room—now! □

I have not had a direct answer to my question. The representative of the Soviet Union says that the official answer of the U.S.S.R. was a statement carried by Tass that it does not need to locate missiles in Cuba. I agree—the U.S.S.R. does not need to. But the question is not whether the U.S.S.R. *needs* missiles in Cuba; the question is: *Has* the U.S.S.R. missiles in Cuba? And that question remains unanswered. I knew it would remain unanswered.

As to the authenticity of the photographs which Mr. Zorin has spoken about with such scorn, I wonder if the Soviet Union would ask its Cuban colleague to permit a United Nations team to go to these sites. If so, Mr. Zorin, I can assure you that we can direct them to the proper places very quickly.

And now I hope that we can get down to business, that we can stop this sparring. We know the facts and so do you, sir, and we are ready to talk about them. Our job here is not to score debating points. Our job, Mr. Zorin, is to save the peace. And if you are ready to try, we are.

REVERSING HISTORICAL FATALITIES *From a speech in New York, March 2, 1961.*

I believe that what is happening, day by day, at the United Nations is just about the most challenging, the most original, even the most exhilarating work being done by men today.

Let us get the perspective straight. In the second half of this twentieth century, we are living through an historical experience which, in all the annals of man, has proved desperately difficult. This experience is the disintegration of one pattern of imperial power and the establishment of new political facts and relationships and power centers in its place. Whenever such changes occur—the really big changes which resemble some vast seismic disturbance in the earth's political crust—the inevitable outcome is disorder, catastrophe, civil conflict and war.

Europe lapsed into barbarism after the fall of Rome. Britain's advance into India followed the crumbling and collapse of the Mogul Empire. In China, where man's longest documented record covers the fortunes of his oldest continuous body politic, the rise and fall of imperial dynasties has a rhythm of almost majestic fatality, each new empire rising on the anarchy and ruins of the last and then, in its own turn, falling away.

Times of imperial collapse are always times of trouble. And we are living through the greatest of such disintegrations today. In less than a generation, the dominion which Western Europe exercised over most of Asia and Africa until the morrow of the Second World War has all but vanished. All Asia has emerged from colonial or semi-colonial control. Africa is in the violent throes of the same process. I doubt if empire on such a scale has ever ended at such breakneck speed. If history is our guide, so rapid and so vast a disintegration must bring the risk of confusion thrice confounded.

And history leaves us in little doubt about the kind of disorder we are likely to endure. We may expect to see new powers jostling to take over the influence and control of the outgoing imperial governments. We may expect to see such efforts sparking local violence and driving it in an outward spiral toward general war. And we may expect, behind local crises and dangers, a general deterioration in international good will, a general increase in distrust and hostility.

Such dangers have marked the collapse of empire before. They mark it now.

So the turbulence we see day by day in the world at large, and reflected back to us through the United Nations, is neither surprising nor new. We should and must expect it. And we must get used to it—we who suffer from having had things our way for so long, we are shocked and hurt when other people don't share our views or question our motives. We judge ourselves by our motives, others by their actions.

What *is* both surprising and new is what the United Nations is trying to *do* about these risks. Now we come to the wholly new chapter in history, the chapter that gives us at least a marginal hope of escaping the dread fatalities of earlier days. To me, I confess, it is a matter of exhilaration that here, here in America, in the newest of continents and in the midst of perhaps the most far-reaching experiment in free unimperial government, a new start should be under way in the management of human affairs, a new experiment to defeat and annihilate the set historical patterns and deadlocks of the past.

Here at the United Nations, the effort *is* being made to confront the old fatalities of collapsing empires and put in their place wholly new approaches to the dilemmas of our time. It is only when we realize how new they are, how radical, how revolutionary, that we can have any idea of the potential value, the profound historical significance of what is being attempted at the United Nations.

For what we are attempting to do today at the United Nations is to roll back every one of the great historical fatalities which, in the past, have made the ending of empire the most perilous condition for the survival of society. We are trying to end the dreary cycle of imperialisms by which the outgoing masters are quickly replaced by new ones who come quickly in to fill the vacuum of power.

The principle which President Wilson declared has since become one of mankind's greatest aspirations—the self-determination of peoples. In the Western world, in this century, the attempt has been made for the first time in history to outlaw imperialism.

This is new. Like all new things, it is difficult. But at least in the last decade, as we have seen the United Nations grow, we must admit that for millions of God's children a first step toward freedom has been taken—the step which recognizes their right, their inalienable right to be free.

But then the dangers and the dilemmas press in. We have done something new in proclaiming the right of small peoples not to be run by other, more powerful states. We have decreed and welcomed the end of colonialism. Indeed, it was in these United States that the first practical steps were taken to raise the principle of anticolonialism from a hope to a fact. The shot that echoed round the world from Lexington echoes on to this day.

But have we ensured that our new faith can be fully and irrevocably expressed in works? Hitherto, as I have said, the ending of one imperialism has usually spelled, for the small and the weak, the beginning of a new. Are we doing better today? The principle may be new. Is the practice equally so?

This to me is the most urgent issue at stake in Africa today. Do the new nations, sometimes irresolute, sometimes wobbly, know how much they need us

Stevenson with advisors at the United Nations. The listening device carries simultaneous translation of foreign-language speeches.

in their period of transition to genuine independence? Or are they blinded by their new nationalism, their hatred of the colonialism of the past, both of which are so skillfully exploited by the propaganda of others who are not trying to help them achieve genuine independence and stability? Was it Alexander Hamilton who said that even to be neutral required a stable government? And Wilson warned us that "Liberty is not itself government. In the wrong hands, in hands unpracticed, undisciplined, it is incompatible with government."

The old colonial system is crumbling and, clearly, only one body can prevent the ancient fatality of simply swapping one control for another. It is the United Nations, consulting closely with its Afro-Asian members, and barring outside intervention from whatever side.

This is our first aim—to put a genuine end to outside imperial control. Our second stems from it—to prevent local disputes from spiraling into general war. Here, again, we do not have to look far back into history to see the kind of tragedy we must, at all costs, avert.

At the turn of the last century, Turkish imperial power crumbled in the Balkans. Czarist Russia on the one hand, Austria-Hungary on the other, pressed in to take its place. In the small, emergent Balkan states, local factions looked to Moscow or Vienna, as in Africa today they may look to Moscow or Paris or Brussels or Washington. The defeat of local Balkan leaders began to take on the aspect of a defeat for the powers which backed them. Two small local wars were contained. Then, in 1914, a bullet killed an archduke, and men stood helplessly by and watched until all the world was engulfed in the horrors of war.

Africa is the Balkans of today. Any outside power seeking to manipulate its griefs and searchings and first fumbling efforts to stand alone risks bringing down on Africa and on the world the dread possibility of nuclear destruction. Is this really what Mr. Khrushchev had in mind when he demanded the withdrawal of the United Nations force and suggested instead that the Congo should become, as the Balkans once were, the cockpit, first of rival factions, then of rival interventions and finally of a spreading, consuming, horrifying general conflict? I cannot believe that any statesman conscious of the dread brink upon which all humanity stands can seek to widen the crisis.

I know it is not easy to reverse the fatalities of history. We are on a melancholy road which again and again mankind has trodden flat with legions of men marching to destruction. In the Congo, in Laos, potentially in any area of conflict and civil disturbance, almost nothing is new. The conflicts are old, the rival suspicions and jockeyings for position are old, the brute struggle for power is as old as man himself. And we know where they have always led—to war and death.

But today one thing *is* new. It is the United Nations' effort to attempt to apply peaceful procedures and rational solutions even to the most aggravated and envenomed of political crises. On a dark scene, in a dark time of troubles, New York's guest, the United Nations, is proclaiming by deed as well as word that men can live, not by violence and brute strength, but, at last, by reason and law.

CAN DEMOCRACY PREVAIL? *From a speech delivered in New York, January 22, 1963.*

As an ex-politician and a practicing diplomat—although many would doubt-less dissent from both of these claims—let me say that when it comes to faith in democracy, I refuse to take a back seat even for my distinguished predecessors on this platform. Because I believe in democracy and freedom, and I believe in their ultimate triumph with the fundamentalist fervor of a survivor of Valley Forge or a Presidential campaign—not to mention two! As Macauley said of Lord Brough-am, or vice versa, "I wish I was as sure of anything as he is of everything." Well, the one thing I'm sure of is that constitutional democracy is that form of govern-ment which best fulfills the nature of man. Moreover, my faith, I remind you, has survived some rather disillusioning experiences.

That's why I'm so glad to be here among people of like conviction who are trying so hard to make freedom and democracy working realities. And that's why I toil in the tangled vineyards of the United Nations, where the leaders of the whole world are trying to practice parliamentary democracy on a global scale.

Bernard Shaw said that democracy was a device that ensures we shall be governed no better than we deserve. The Center for the Study of Democratic Institutions, as I understand it, can be thought of, then, as a kind of national insurance plan, a way of making certain that we will deserve better and better.

For years Robert Hutchins talked about the need for a democratic version of the Platonic Academy, to deal with new questions of freedom and justice as they emerged on the changing horizon of our times. Finally, with the establishment of the Center, his dream came true. Now I gather from a few delicate hints that the time has come to think about an endowment policy for this insurance plan, and I am pleased to lend my endorsement to what the Center has already done and promises to do in the years ahead. For busy, battered bureaucrat though I be, I am a staunch believer in the leisure of the theory class.

Ten years ago last July, as Governor of Illinois, I welcomed the Democratic national convention to Chicago. And I hope you will forgive me for resurrecting some of my words.

"This is not the time for superficial solutions and everlasting elocution," I said in 1952, "nor for frantic boast and foolish word. . . . Self-criticism is the secret weapon of democracy. . . . We dare not just look back on great yesterdays. We must look forward to great tomorrows. What counts now is not just what we are *against*, but what we are *for*. *Who* leads us is less important than *what* leads us—what convictions, what courage, what faith."

I should like to think that these words apply to the Center for the Study of Democratic Institutions and the work that goes on there. For we have all learned that modern technology can strengthen the despot's hand and the dictator's grasp, and for that reason, if no other, we know that democracy is more necessary now than it ever was.

Of course, democracy is not self-executing. We have to make it work, and to make it work we have to understand it. Sober thought and fearless criticism are impossible without critical thinkers and thinking critics. Such persons must be given the opportunity to come together, to see new facts in the light of old principles, to evaluate old principles in the light of new facts, and by deliberation, debate and dialogue to hammer out the consensus that makes democracy possible. And this, as we all know well, though some of us forget from time to time, requires intellectual independence, impenitent speculation and freedom from political pressure. In a word, it requires centers of the kind found on Eucalyptus Hill in Santa Barbara.

And I hope the day may come when such centers are multiplied the world over. For democracy's need for wisdom will remain as perennial as its need for liberty. Not only external vigilance but unending self-examination must be the perennial price of liberty, because the work of self-government never ceases. The work of an institution like the Center, therefore, is similar to the work of the church in this regard—it will be required as long as final salvation eludes us, which will be until the end of time.

The study of democratic institutions—how to create them, how to sustain them, how to preserve them—will be necessary as long as men continue to seek faith in themselves, continue to harbor hope in their own capacity for progress and cherish the charity that unites them in a common cause.

And with a world undergoing such rapid change in geography, politics and economics, the need to adapt our old and venerated institutions to the changes is urgent.

Ten years ago, Robert Oppenheimer said: "In an important sense, this world of ours is a new world, in which the unity of knowledge, the nature of human communities, the order of society, the order of ideas, the very notions of society and culture have changed, and will not return to what they have been in the past. . . . The world alters as we walk in it, so that the years of man's life measure not some small growth or rearrangement or moderation of what he has learned in childhood, but a great upheaval."

I suppose whether democracy can prevail in the great upheaval of our time is a valid question. Certainly, after 150 years of uninterrupted expansion of the idea of government by consent of the governed, it has recently met with mounting and formidable challenges all over the world from Fascist, Nazi, Communist authoritarians and a variety of dictatorships. And we have good reason to know how clumsy, slow, inefficient and costly it is compared to the celerity, certainty and secrecy of absolutism.

But the important thing is that it *has* survived. The important thing is that even the absolutists masquerade as democrats; even the military and quasi-military dictatorships strive in the name of democracy to manage the public business. And all of them say that authoritarianism is only a necessary transition to democracy.

Why? Because it is the most popular form of government yet devised; because it is, as it always has been, not only the prize of the steadfast and the courageous, but the privilege of those who are better off; because, in short, as Jefferson said,

Adlai Stevenson and Eleanor Roosevelt at the United Nations.

it is "the only form of government which is not eternally at open or secret war with the rights of the people."

I have therefore no doubt that, distant as it may be for many people, it will ultimately prevail, that it will rewin lost ground, that it will expand its dominion, that it can withstand the wild winds that are blowing through the world if—and I repeat if—we who are its custodians continually re-examine and adapt its principles to the changing needs of our changing times.

Years ago, Reinhold Niebuhr observed that "man's capacity for justice makes democracy possible; but man's inclination to injustice makes democracy necessary."

And I suppose that most of us, if we were asked to name the most profound issues at stake in the world today, would say the issues of freedom and democracy. We would say that the Western world, for all its errors and shortcomings, has for centuries tried to evolve a society in which the individual has enough legal, social and political elbow room to be, not the puppet of the community, but his own autonomous self.

And we would say that the enemies of freedom, whatever the magnificent ends they propose—the brotherhood of man, the kingdom of saints, "from each according to his ability, to each according to his needs"—miss just this essential point: that man is greater than the social purposes to which he can be put. He must not be kicked about even with the most high-minded objectives. He is not a means or an instrument. He is an end in himself.

This, I take it, is the essence of what we mean by democracy—not so much voting systems or parliamentary systems or economic or legal systems (though they all enter in) as an irrevocable and final dedication to the dignity of man. In this sense, democracy is perhaps mankind's most audacious experiment. This dignity and equality of the human person could hardly be further removed from the existential facts of human existence. There is precious little dignity or equality in our natural state.

Most human beings have to spend their lives in utter vulnerability. All are murderable and torturable and survive only through the restraint shown by more powerful neighbors. All are born unequal, in terms of capacity or strength. All are born to the inherent frailty of the human condition, naked and helpless, vulnerable all through life to the will of others, limited by ignorance, limited by physical weakness, limited by fear, limited by the phobias that fear engenders.

For nearly three thousand years now, the political and social genius of what we can permissibly call "Western man" has struggled with these brute facts of our unsatisfactory existence. Ever since the Hebrews discovered personal moral responsibility and the Greeks discovered the autonomy of the citizen, the effort has been made—with setbacks and defeats, with dark ages and interregnums and any number of irrelevant adventures on the side—to create a social order in which weak, fallible, obstinate, silly, magnificent man can maintain his dignity and exercise his free and responsible choice.

The task has never been easy. Each step has been a groping in the dark—the dark of violence and brute power and overweening arrogance. Yet we have learned some of the preconditions and expedients of freedom. And we have incorporated them in societies and institutions. What we seek to defend today against new critics and new adversaries is essentially a great body of *experience*, not theories or untried ideals, but a solid mass of lived-through facts. First in time came the great medieval discovery that the king must be subject to the law.

Equality before the law has been expanded and safeguarded by consultation and representation—in other words, the vote. This is not simply a device for peacefully changing government, although it is that, too. It is not only a means of allowing the wearer to say where the shoe pinches. It is, in addition, a means of offsetting the natural inequalities which grow up in any society, however organized, as a result of the unequal endowment of people.

The head of, say, General Electric, has more means of influencing society than a small-town electrician. Against the advantages of brains and money, the vote is the only advantage the small man has. His voice, or vote, added to millions of other voices, offsets the accumulated power of society's entrenched positions.

But equality before the law and at the ballot box are only strands in the seamless robe in which all our liberties are woven together. Carelessly unravel one and the robe itself may come apart.

Another is enough social and economic opportunity for each man, even the poorest, to hold his dignity intact. The widest access to education and training, equal opportunity for talent to find its niche, security of income and work, the chances of health—all these belong to a social order of responsible and respected citizens. We no longer define democracy solely in political terms. The great effort of this century has been to work out its economic and social implications.

If we take these three main strands of democracy—equality before the law, constitutional representative government and social and economic opportunity —it is clear that they face, as evolving free society has always faced, new challenges in our own day. It is profoundly concerned with the extension of the concept of democracy—extension in depth, for we now believe that no human being, however lowly his occupation or poor his resources, can be excluded from the dignity of man—extension in space, for the whole world is now a community and we have to find ways in which the idea of a truly human society can be realized on a planetary scale. The two processes, going forward simultaneously in every part of the globe, make up the vast revolutionary ferment of our day.

What we have to attempt today is the building of intercontinental forms of free community—certainly the most testing experiment of all those made so far by free men. Yet our past achievements give us the right to hope for future success.

One form of association already exists between virtually all the nations of this globe and, whatever work we may accomplish on a regional basis, progress at the United Nations in the direction of a free society of equals must be part of our effort to extend the principle of liberty as the essential working principle of mankind.

How are we to set about this task? There is one method which, I most profoundly hope, we shall avoid, and that is the method of self-righteous exhortation.

We have, I fear, sometimes displayed an unattractive tendency to lecture new governments on their constitutional shortcomings and to point, sometimes openly, sometimes implicitly, to the superior performance of the West.

We can admit that free government *is* a Western invention—by all odds, its finest political achievement. But there are several things we must remember as well. We must remember that it took about eight centuries to develop these patterns of life in our own culture. We must remember that our form of democracy is the most subtle and sophisticated form of government in the world; other, more primitive, still developing peoples cannot be expected to master it over-night. But move toward it they will, and such institutions as the United Nations help to train their leadership in our ways. Moreover, new states always face appalling problems of readjustment, and we must be smart enough to recognize when and how these alien leaderships move our way.

If now we see in Africa single-party rule dominated by one leader, with changing policies and political choice severely restricted, we should not hold up our hands in horror, but remember that this is not far from our politics of two centuries ago.

Where we have every right to express our alarm is in the breakdown of constitutional protection by the law. The danger lies not so much in parliamentary failure as in judicial failure. Yet, even here, our alarm should be expressed in modest terms. In eighteenth-century England, a man could be hanged for stealing a sheep, and horrible ships took convicts to Australia for no more than petty larceny. Nor was Europe's recent Fascism precisely a law-abiding mode of government.

No—the way ahead does not lie through sermonizing carried on by people whose own eyes are too full of beams to judge clearly the others' motes. It lies rather in a sustained effort to work out, within the United Nations and in partner-ships with other nations, the chief lines of advance toward a more coherent and viable world community, with freedom as its working principle and constitu-tionalism as its political habit. No one is likely to underestimate the appalling complexities of the task. But the outlook must have seemed as daunting to the lawyers struggling against Stuart despotism or the Founding Fathers attempting to turn federalism into a workable system.

The task is indeed "piled high with difficulty." We should attempt it, there-fore, with all the more vigor and clarity, and I would suggest that the three criteria I stressed in domestic democracy are relevant, too, to the global democ-racy we painfully must try to build.

Today, the first of all tasks is to restrain the nation-state from taking law into its own hands—in other words, from using force to assert its will—or, in the final word, from making war.

From domestic society, we know the only way to banish lawless violence and fratricidal strife is by accepting rules of peaceful change and adjustment and building an impartial police force to enforce the peaceful solutions that are agreed. This I take to be a task of the United Nations. However, no world body can yet take on the tasks of global peace. Some of our vast modern states are still, like the medieval barons, too powerful to be controlled in their feudal fastnesses.

But perhaps we have reached a first stage of restraint on arbitrary power. Troubled areas—Palestine, the Congo, Laos—are policed, not by rivals whose rivalry would lead to war, but by an external and impartial third force.

Could we not extend the principle? Could we not aim at the policing by the United Nations of more and more areas in which the rival interests of powerful states threaten to clash? Global systems of restraint may still evade us. But history suggests we can start from the particular instance and then extend the principle, and every area withdrawn from the naked arbitrament of force is an area saved for the constitutional working of a sane human society.

Does the second principle I have picked out—the procedure of equal voting —apply to the building of a free world society? The critics say the new states, holding the balance of power by means of their combined vote, drive the United Nations on toward ferocious extremes of anticolonialism and attempt to impose other imprudent policies on the Great Powers which must disrupt the whole organization. Meanwhile, the great foot the bill.

There is much to be said on this score. For the moment, let me only say that in world society, the small nation, like the small man in domestic society, is most likely to be vulnerable. His equal voice, his capacity to unite it with other small voices, is a measure of protection against his inequality. We see the need for this countervailing power inside our states. So let us not be too quick to denounce it in the world at large.

There is a further reason for being cautious and patient about the workings inside the United Nations of the potential ex-colonial majority. If we turn to the third principle of democracy—equality of esteem, equal dignity, equal access to the social and economic possibilities of society—we find that the disproportions which distort true community inside our states are present in world society, too. This Afro-Asian bloc—a misnomer, for, save on the colonial issue, there is no bloc—represents most of the world's most truly underprivileged peoples. If they cling to their United Nations status, it is because, as citizens of our planet, they have not yet much else to cling to. Pushed to the first outskirts of modernity by Western investment and trade, emancipated before they had received either the training or the powers of wealth-creation needed for a modern society, they are caught between two worlds—the powerful, affluent, expanding world of the developed "North" and the traditional, pretechnological, largely poor world of the underdeveloped "South."

This division in world society is a great obstacle to the expansion of the confidence and community the world needs for a truly human society. And it threatens to become worse if such experiments as the European Common Market or the Atlantic Community prove to be, vis-à-vis the less fortunate parts of the world, a rich man's club, exclusive in its commerce, its investments, its arrangements and its interests. The gap exists. We must not make it worse.

What can we do? I would like to suggest that we, the wealthiest, most fortunate of all the developed states of the "North," have two lines to follow, both of them essential if we in this generation are to make our full contribution to the advance of world democracy.

I know there is much dissatisfaction about aid, much feeling that it is wasted and never achieves a breakthrough, and dribbles away down thousands of unspecified drains and ratholes. Yet just so did the Victorians talk about tax money devoted to lifting the standards of the very poor in early industrial society. There were the "good poor" who said "Please" and "Thank you" and touched their forelocks. Then there were the "bad poor" who kept coal in the bathtub. But over a couple of generations, it was the raising of all this unfortunate mass of humanity that turned Western society into the first social order in history in which everyone could expect something of an equal chance.

After ten years, we are only at the beginning of the experiment of international aid. We are learning greatly. We see the relevance of some policies, the supreme obstacles offered by others. We discriminate more. We are learning to be better givers.

Our second task is harder. It is harder for us than for any other member of the world's wealthy elite. It is to see that the last vestiges of discrimination inside our own society are speedily abolished. It is no use talking of ourselves as the vanguard of freedom and democracy while any of our fellow Americans can be treated like a James Meredith at the University of Mississippi.

Must we not, as lovers of freedom and as—too often—self-styled prophets of the free way of life, sometimes lapse into a shamed silence when we even have to talk about social injustice, let alone deal with it—one hundred years after the Emancipation Proclamation?

I must end as I began. The essence of democracy is the dignity of man. We shall create a free world order on no other basis. If we attack communism—as we must—for its contempt for political dignity, we must attack as unrelentingly lapses in social dignity.

It sometimes seems to me today as though, through all the great issues of the day—the anticolonial revulsion, the political contest with communism, the unification of Europe, the clamor of poorer lands for advance—there runs the underlying desire for some lasting realization of the dignity of man; man with a measure of political autonomy, man with the economic elbow room to live above the torturing doubts of food and work, man with the dignity to look his neighbor in the face and see a friend.